Country Houses
in
Great Britain

Yale Center for British Art
New Haven

Front cover: 3. Jan Siberechts, WOLLATON HALL AND PARK, NOTTING-
HAMSHIRE, 1697 (Detail)

This catalogue commemorates an exhibition at the Yale Center for British Art, New
Haven, October 10, 1979 – January 13, 1980. It was compiled by Mary Spivy, Ellen
D'Oench and Joy Breslauer, under the supervision of Malcolm Cormack.

Design: Heidi Humphrey
Production Supervision: Yale University Printing Service

Preface

This exhibition is one of a series mounted in the Yale Center for British Art from the richness of its own resources. Previous exhibitions have been *Seascapes, Wildlife in British Art* and *The British View of India*. The intention behind the exhibition has been to examine closely some of the Center's collection of topographical views, in particular those of country houses and their gardens. Paul Mellon has written elsewhere about his own love of the English countryside and its houses, so that it is not surprising that the collection is rich in such works. The recent success of books on this theme demonstrates an interest which the show hopes further to promote and satisfy. Paintings of towns, ruined castles and general topographical views, while not included, are available for further study in the Center's other galleries.

Henry James, on a visit to Warwick Castle, found it the model of a great dwelling "which amply satisfies the imagination without irritating the democratic conscience" *(English Hours,* ed. Alma Louis Lowe, London, 1960, p. 55). Whatever political or social solution is found to preserve these monuments of a past society, the exhibition aims to show the variety of art and skills which produced and recorded these important examples of a cultural heritage and thereby bring them to a wider public.

The major part of the work on the exhibition has been produced in the Department of Paintings, under the supervision of its curator. Mary Spivy, a graduate student from Williams College, Joy Breslauer, Curatorial Assistant, and Ellen D'Oench, Assistant Curator, provided the draft entries, and, in addition, Mary Spivy wrote the draft introduction. Without their enthusiasm and hard work the exhibition would not have been possible. They received much useful information and help from colleagues in the Center, particularly Andrew Wilton, Curator of Prints and Drawings and Joan Friedman, Curator of Rare Books, and the staff of their departments. From outside the Center, Beverly Carter, John Harris, Curator of Prints and Drawings, Royal Institute of British Architects, and David Davies-Cook also provided invaluable assistance. The department acknowledges a general debt to earlier pioneers in the subject, such as Christopher Hussey and John Cornforth and their writings.

The exhibition has been divided into paintings, drawings and watercolors, prints and books, arranged chronologically within each section. In the catalogue, various abbreviations which recur often have been listed separately and in all measurements, height precedes width and inches are given before centimeters. Details of provenance, previous exhibitions and bibliography have been given only for the paintings. There is an index of the places and artists represented in the exhibition.

Malcolm Cormack
Curator of Paintings

Introduction

"France has her chateaux, Italy has her historic villas. . . . Germany her robber castles, but the exact equivalent of what we mean by the English country house is not to be found elsewhere. It may be large, it may be small; it may be palatial, it may be manorial; it may be of stone, brick, stucco, or even beams and plaster; it may be the seat of the aristocracy or the home of the gentry- whatever it is, it possesses "one outstanding characteristic: it is the English country house."

Vita Sackville-West,
English Country Houses
(London, 1944) p. 7

The exhibition attempts to show what was meant by the English country house and how it was represented. The paintings, drawings, prints and books range in date and medium from a large bird's eye oil painting of Llannerch, a Welsh country seat (ca. 1662) by an unknown provincial artist to a watercolor of Osborne House (ca. 1845) given to Queen Victoria and Prince Albert as a presentation piece by the architect, Thomas Cubitt. The variety of works document changes that occurred, not only in architecture and garden design, but also in the artistic interpretation of the country house, as the vision of the artist and the taste of the patron shifted over a two hundred year period. All encompassing bird's-eye views were popular in the seventeenth century, but lost favor in the early eighteenth century as a new attitude toward nature and life itself became apparent. In the late eighteenth and early nineteenth centuries, picturesque and romantic landscapes became more important than a careful topographic rendering of the house. The variety of intentions can be seen in the exhibition. Some paintings no doubt were extremely accurate, for example Siberechts's view of *Wollaton Hall* (Cat. 3), but others such as the Philips painting of the *Finch Family* (Cat. 13), seem rather to commemorate attitudes of taste, with imaginary buildings that existed only in the minds of the patrons. Devis in his view of *Okeover Hall* (Cat. 15) attempted to reproduce the exact wishes of the owner but, unfortunately, the house was not built as painted. In his view of *Atherton Hall* (Cat. 16), however, he is more accurate than contempory prints of the house which were published.

Books merit special attention because of the part they played in the dissemination of increasing knowledge in gardens and gardening and in houses and architectural style. Their existence signified from the Renaissance onward the growth of civilized living with the interest in the arts and humanism. John Gerard's *Herball* (1597), John Parkinson's *Paradisi in Sole, Paradisus Terrestris* (1629) and John Lawson's *A New Orchard and Garden* (1618) were important treatises for the country house owner interested in devising a garden suitable for his residence and his position. The landed gentleman improved his education through the study of architecture, literature, art and poetry and knowledge of gardening was equally important. He consulted architectural pattern books such as Sebastiano Serlio's *Venetian Quarto* containing Books I–VI (1566) and *The First and Chief Groundes of Architecture* (1563) by John Shute.

Two books published in 1715 had an important influence on country house design. One was the first volume of *Vitruvius Britannicus* by Colen Campbell, a folio size book illustrating facades and elevations of classical buildings in England. The other, a translation of Palladio's *I Quattro libri dell'architettura,* was to revolutionize taste, although his work had been known in England since Inigo Jones returned from Italy around 1615. Country house builders and owners turned, not only to these architectural pattern books and theoretical works, but also to garden designers for ideas and plans for the improvement of their properties. Batty Langley published the *New Principles of Gardening* in 1728 and Humphrey Repton wrote several notable treatises in the early nineteenth century. A book of views, *Britannia Illustrata,* provided further inspiration for houses and gardens in Britain and on the Continent. It first appeared in 1707 and was subsequently revised and reprinted, sometimes in French translation (see Cat. 97). The folio size publication of engravings by Johannes Kip after paintings and drawings by Leonard Knyff, [see, for example, *Chiswick* (Cat. 50)], was popular among the French and English aristocracy. Through these publications, they could see the latest trends in house and garden design and perhaps plan a trip to see some of the most famous country seats. These books were essential for the diffusion of ideas and trends that created the English country house and garden.

The first boom in country house building occurred during the Tudor period as the threat of internal strife had receded and a more civilized way of life was established. The plan of these houses developed out of two prototypes. On the one hand were the castles, introduced by the French after the Norman conquest of 1066 as the first large scale domestic buildings in England, and on the other the abbeys and priories, built consistently since the eleventh century by various religious groups. Out of such defensive and ecclesiastical buildings, the country house emerged. Two important forces influenced the shift from castle and priory to private house. These were the decrease of religious domination after the Reformation over all phases of social and political life and an increase in the political and economic power of the aristocracy which fluctuated with the whims of Queen Elizabeth I. The labor force, which was formerly dedicated to building churches, had its efforts transferred to domestic structures after the dissolution of the monasteries between 1533 and 1539 under Henry VIII. The court and wealthy layman competed with the church as the major patrons. A country seat may then have been called Castle, Hall, Court, House, Manor, Abbey, or Priory when, for example, religious lands had been made over to private owners as gifts for political support.

The large "Prodigy" houses of the Elizabethan period were built on great tracts of land owned by the nobility and members of the political elite. The urge for power and money usually resulted in the aggrandizement or the purchase of a country seat. Prestige and income were dependent on the size of the estate and the number of paying tenant farmers. The seat was an agricultural center as well as a place to entertain royalty and friends. The Queen visited the lavish houses belonging to members of her court on her regular progressions around the kingdom. Many houses, such as *Wollaton Hall* (see Cat. 3) and *Hampton Court, Herefordshire* (see Cats. 4, 5, & 6), were altered to become grander, more modern, and more impressive to attract the royal presence.

Owners of large houses such as Sir Thomas Willoughby of Wollaton and Lord Coningsby of Hampton Court, Herefordshire, having built these vast structures, would commission artists to paint views of their properties. The house picture, as with individual portraiture, which had become increasingly popular in the sixteenth century, documented the family's wealth and prestige. The bird's-eye view was used more frequently than any other vantage point in seventeenth-century British country house portraits. The odd viewpoint, which simulates that of a man in a balloon, could show the full extent of the owner's land and therefore suggest his dominant position in society. This way of depicting a house and garden had become uncommon in continental Europe by the seventeenth century. Many artists, both Dutch and Flemish, were striving toward a more naturalistic approach. Some attempted to follow the example of Rubens's painting of his own country house, the Chateau de Steen, with its attention to detail and baroque sweep. The bird's-eye view was an older style last used around 1598 by the Netherlandish artist Giusto Utens for lunette paintings of Medici houses and gardens, such as those for the Villa Artimino, near Florence. The odd perspective was re-introduced by Floris van Berkerode who, in his 1631 engraving of the palace of Prince Henry, "married the techniques of cartography with architectural drawing and engraving" (Harris 1978, p. 1821). The Bohemian artist Wenceslaus Hollar in his 1659 view of Windsor Castle and Jacob Knyff of the Netherlands in his 1673 painting of Durdans in Surrey, reverted to the bird's-eye view which was also used by other Netherlandish artists, such as Danckerts, Knyff and Siberechts. They had gone to England and became specialists in country house portraiture which demanded this style. Siberechts was well skilled in the natural landscape style of Rubens and Dutch artists, but abandoned it soon after coming to England around 1674. There is no definite documented reason why the English landowner rejected the new Netherlandish style in favor of an older outmoded form. Perhaps he liked the bird's-eye view because it showed in the simplest way the full extent of his domination over nature or, that it rendered, as he recorded his other possessions, his family, his horses, most accurately. The reason also may have something to do with the seventeenth-century practice of surveying the countryside from a raised terrace of an elevated banqueting house to gain a bird's-eye view of the flat parterres and knot gardens laid out like a patterned carpet below. In most portraits of this period, such as *Denham Place* (Cat. 7), *Bayhall* (Cat. 2), *Wollaton* (Cat. 3) and *Hampton Court, Herefordshire* (Cats. 4,5&6), the massive bulk of the house dominated the landscape. There is a marked contrast between the cultivated garden and fields around the house and the vast wild areas beyond. Perhaps the country house builder wanted the achievement of this control over the landscape commemorated in a bird's-eye view portrait. Certainly, the portrait of the house was more important than the memory of the artist, if the number of anonymous views is any indication.

In the early eighteenth century, the idea of man's control over nature exemplified by the large scale bird's-eye view paintings changed to one of man's enjoyment of and participation in nature.

Instead of viewing the formal garden from above, the country house owner wanted to walk or drive through the revised garden and park to appreciate its pleasures at ground level. This change in eye level is also apparent in painting. There is a movement away from the cartographical renderings of the seventeenth century toward a naturalistic landscape view. The painting of *Bifrons Park* (Cat. 10) to some extent documents this transition. The artist is on the same level as the hunting party and looks back toward the house in a modified bird's-eye view. Although the garden is still walled off from the surrounding countryside, the house no longer dominates the landscape but becomes a part of it more in keeping with the Dutch tradition.

The actual size of the painting changed in the early eighteenth century. Large size pictures, like *Denham Place* (Cat. 7) and *Wollaton Hall* (Cat. 3) were not totally abandoned, but there was a general trend toward smaller, more intimate paintings in which the house served as a backdrop for human activities or was incorporated into the landscape view. This change of scale, incidentally, brought about a change in perspective and viewpoint. The larger paintings of the seventeenth century were generally meant to be seen from below and would have been hung high on the wall. Different means besides the bird's-eye view were used to depict the country house. The house picture and the family portrait were combined to create the conversation piece, such as Arthur Devis's paintings of the *Gwillym Family* (Cat. 16) and *Leak Okeover* (Cat. 15) in front of Okeover Hall. In both works, the country house owner stands proudly in the well-kept landscape surrounding his house. The sporting picture, in which the house is combined with the portraits of animals or people hunting, became popular. Leonard Knyff's *Black Game* (Cat. 8) and *Hon. Marcia and Hon. George Pitt, Riding in the Park of Stratfield Saye House, Hampshire* by Thomas Gooch (Cat. 28) exemplify this type, with the house relegated to the background.

The paintings themselves look different, just as the houses and gardens depicted in them do not resemble the great Elizabethan "Prodigy" estates. There was a movement toward smaller and more livable houses in the eighteenth century. More people, not necessarily noblemen, could afford to build and to buy country property. The paintings of *Kidbrooke Park* (Cat. 23) and *Mount Kennedy* (Cat. 27) show houses of a more practical and human scale. Owners continued to build large houses but the style of architecture had changed. The Palladian and classical ideal exemplified by a symmetrical block-like building, a pedimented and columned temple front, rusticated lower floor and simple decoration became the new rule. Pattern books such as *Vitruvius Britannicus* (Cat. 98) depicted classical buildings and thus encouraged enthusiasm for the new style. The paintings of *Powerscourt* (Cat. 21) and *Atherton Hall*(Cat. 16) and the drawings of *Chatsworth* (Cat. 62), *Wanstead* (Cat. 81), and *Harewood* (Cats. 74&75) show houses in the Palladian mode. This interest in classical architecture brought with it a feeling for idealized landscape both in painting and in nature. Nevertheless, a more intimate style also progressed. Areas around London were slowly developed with modest country houses close to the amenities of the city. Twickenham and Richmond were popular as early suburbs; the poet Alexander Pope and the politician and garden enthusiast James Johnston owned houses in these districts (see the paintings attributed to Joseph Nickolls, (Cats. 17&18).

For some artists, the depiction of the house in a closer architectural rendering was not as important as the depiction of the landscape. In the *View of Wilton House* (ca. 1760)(Cat. 20) by Richard Wilson, a topographical or architecturally accurate view of the house is clearly subordinated to the idealized Claudian landscape.

Wilson was not alone in this. Gainsborough's celebrated reply to Lord Hardwicke, who had asked for a view of his house, is well known;

> "Paul Sandby is the only Man of Genius, he believes, who has employed his Pencil that Way—Mr G. hopes Lord Hardwicke will not mistake his meaning, but if His Lordship wishes to have anything tollerable [sic] of the name of G. the Subject altogether, as well as figures &c must be of his own Brain . . ."

> (Gainsborough to Lord Hardwicke, not dated, Mary Woodall, *The Letters of Thomas Gainsborough*, London, 2nd edition, 1963, no. 42, pp. 87 and 91).

With John Constable and J.M.W. Turner, the demands of their artistic vision and aesthetic ideals sometimes meant the subordination of strict topography. The *Hampton Court, Herefordshire* watercolors (Cats. 78&79) are, however, accurate but with a freshness and sparkle that comes from Turner's interpretation of the landscape around them. John Constable, commissioned by Henry Lewis to paint *Malvern Hall* around 1821 (Cat. 36), focused more on the light and atmosphere than on the house itself. Constable himself could also complain to his friend John Fisher, "I do not regret not seeing Fonthill. I never had a desire to see sights—and a gentleman's park is my aversion. It is not beauty because it is not nature . . ." (Oct. 7th, 1822, *John Constable's Correspondence, VI., The Fishers,* ed. R.B. Beckett, Suffolk Records Society, 1968, p.98). One of his most successful works, however, is a view of a house, *Wivenhoe Park* (Washington, National Gallery of Art), although it is fundamentally a landscape of the effects of noon in high summer. In James Ward's painting called *Cattle at a Pool at Sunrise* (Cat. 38), Tabley House is only a minor part of the composition and not the main subject.

The eclecticism of architectural and painting styles in the late eighteenth and early nineteenth centuries shows how varied the attitudes of artists and architects had become. A strict categorization of approach, which is possible in seventeenth-and early eighteenth-century painting and building types, no longer applies. The picturesque style in both architectural and painted creations evolved out of a continued movement toward a natural landscape. It incorporated a search for romance, beauty and mystery, while evoking a revival of earlier and exotic architectural styles. The picturesque house of the early nineteenth century took many forms, of which the Italianate (Cat. 87) and the Athenian villa (Cat. 91) are but two examples. The paintings of *Easby Abbey* (Cat. 30) and *Lee Priory* (Cat. 32) show the return toward a monastic and Gothic style inspired by Horace Walpole's ideas and his own house, Strawberry Hill. The Elizabethan revival is evident in an architectural drawing by C.J. Richardson for a proposed house in the Tudor style in the 1830s (Cat. 93). One of the most exotic styles of the picturesque era was the Indian; it is visible in the sketchbook by Anne Rushout showing *Sezincote House* (Cat. 89) and in the Thomas Daniell painting of the Indian inspired garden there (Cat. 35). In keeping with the eclecticism of painting styles in the nineteenth century is *Tiptree Hall Farm* (Cat. 43), which marks a revival of the bird's-eye view. This painting is also an indication of increasing industrialization and the surge toward modernization in the countryside during the 1850s. The agriculturist John Mechi as owner of the farm had converted his land from a useless swamp into productive acreage using modern methods. The use of modern methods of illustration, such as photography, may have resulted in fewer house portraits in the late nineteenth and twentieth centuries. Although paintings of country seats have been produced in the last hundred years, their number is small in comparison with previous centuries.

Any discussion of the country house itself and its representation in art is not complete or even understandable without a knowledge of the history of the gardens and landscape which surrounded it. The country house owner did not divorce his house from the land and very few artists rendered the country house without at least a suggestion of its surroundings. The house and garden or landscape area were conceived of as an entity and were depicted as such.

The cult of the garden developed in England in the sixteenth century and has continued as an important element of society since that time. In the Tudor period gardens were made as impressive as the houses to attract the attention of the monarchy. Notable men such as William Cecil, Walter Raleigh, Francis Bacon and Francis Carew discussed and participated in the creation of gardens. In 1625, Francis Bacon published an essay called *Of Gardens* which extolled the beauties of nature. It has remained as evidence of the English love of nature since its appearance in the seventeenth century.

> "God almighty first planted a Garden. And indeed, it is the purest of Human Pleasures, It is the Greatest of Human Pleasures. It is the Greatest Refreshment to the Spirit of Man; Without which, Buildings and Palaces are but Gross Handi-works; And a man shall ever see, that when Ages grow to Civility and Elegance, Men will come to Build stately sooner than to Garden finely as if Gardening were the Greater Perfection."

The formal seventeenth century garden in England and on the continent became a carefully organized space whose requirements were set forth in contemporary garden manuals. The garden was to have "a fountain in the midst thereof" and "wide and fair allées" (John Parkinson, *Paradisi in Sole, Paradisus Terrestris*, 1629). There was to be "an orchard full of pleasure and delight" (Lawson, *A New Orchard and Garden*, 1618). A moat or canal would provide "fish, fence, and moisture" (Lawson, 1618) and a banqueting house provided a place from which to view the garden and the passage of the hunt in the fields beyond. These characteristics are visible in the paintings of *Denham Hall* (Cat. 7), *Wollaton* (Cat. 3), and *Hampton Court, Herefordshire* (Cats. 4,5,&6). The typical garden was a large flat of terraced area with geometrically shaped beds defined by hedges, topiary, *allées,* straight canals and sheets of water. The parterres and terraces served as outdoor rooms in a garden that was an extension of the house itself. These ornate spaces were based on French designs like that at Versailles, which were in part inspired by Italian renaissance gardens. The waterworks and statuary were derived from Italy, the sense of grandeur and scale from France and the use of topiary from the Netherlands. Because of its small size and the generous use of potted plants, the garden at Mr. Pierrepont's house (Cat. 11) looks particularly Dutch.

The continental formal garden style prevalent in the seventeenth century gradually went out of favor, as did the use of the bird's-eye view to illustrate it. Changing tastes in gardening, literature, art and poetry were the cause. In the early eighteenth century, with the writings of the third Earl of Shaftsbury and Alexander Pope, a new attitude toward the landscape appears. Their works, along with the later practical efforts of the garden architects Charles Bridgeman, William Kent and Capability Brown, played a large role in the shift toward an aesthetic enjoyment of natural beauties. Shaftsbury praised nature ecstatically in *The Moralists* (1709):

> "O Glorious Nature, supremely Fair, and sovereignly Good! All-loving and All-lovely, All-divine. Whose Looks are so becoming, and of such infinite Grace; whose study brings such Wisdom, and whose Contemplation such Delight; whose every single Work affords an ampler Scene, and is a nobler Spectacle than all that ever Art presented!"

This change in attitude perhaps corresponded to change in political events and social developments. In 1714 after Queen Anne's death, the Hanoverian monarchy under George I succeeded to the British throne. The new Whig government tended to associate French formal gardens with Toryism. The natural landscape style advocated by Addison and Steele in magazines like *The Spectator* and *The Guardian* was equated with liberty and democracy in the modern mind. Other factors which led to this change in taste were more practical in nature. Stag hunting, for example, which required long straight avenues, became less fashionable and fox hunting, which required expansive open land and hilly terrain, became more popular.

The new way of looking at the landscape was expressed by the poet Alexander Pope (1688-1744) in his *Epistle to Lord Burlington*. He applied his ideals to the construction of his own garden at Twickenham, (seen in the painting of his villa, attributed to Joseph Nickolls, Cat. 17):

                    "Tis sense;
           Good sense, which only is the gift of heaven,
        And tho' no Science, fairly worth the Seven,
        A light, which in yourself you must perceive;
        Jones and Le Nôtre have it not to give.
                To build, to plant, whatever you intend,
        To rear the column, or the Arch to bend,
        To swell the Terras, or to sink the Grot;
        In all, let Nature never be forgot.
        . . . Consult the Genius of the Place in all. . . ."

Good sense and an understanding of the natural "Genius of the Place" were necessary to create the new landscape style which rejected formal plans of the seventeenth century, such as those of Inigo Jones and André Le Nôtre. All of nature was to be regarded as a garden, not just the cultivated plants surrounding the house. The fence and wall disappeared from sight, replaced by the Ha-Ha, a sunken ditch which prevented grazing cattle and sheep from coming too near the house, yet allowed an unobstructed view across the countryside. Houses were situated to take advantage of the natural prospects. Hills and views were created if none existed. Terraces and parterres were washed away as the all encompassing landscape swept right up to the house.

Contemporary literature had a great influence on the dissemination of the new style, but classical texts and the paintings of Claude Lorrain and Nicholas Poussin were also important. Country house owners, reading the works of Ovid, Virgil and Homer, attempted to create a similar Arcadia. Englishmen on the Grand Tour saw and bought paintings of the idealized Italian landscape, with classical temples, decaying ruins, and rolling vistas by the seventeenth-century artists. They returned to England with a desire to recreate the classical landscape on British soil. The drawing by Chatelain of the garden at Stowe (cat. 58) is an example of an Italian Arcadia complete with temples, lakes and vistas. Paintings of *Powerscourt* (Cat. 21) and *Mount Kennedy* (Cat. 27) show the classical landscape extending right up to the house.

In the late eighteenth and early nineteenth centuries, the garden style changed with the adoption of picturesque ideals. By 1807, Robert Southey in his *Letters from England* had commented on how necessary it was to take a dose of the picturesque rather in the way one went in search of "a course of spring physic." The writings of William Gilpin, Payne Knight and Uvedale Price were well

14

known among men and women of taste and sensibility. Jane Austen was to satirize such preoccupations in her *Northanger Abbey* (Chap. 14). She realized full well that a contrived way of contemplating nature produced an artificial approach to art. In turn, the landscape itself was changed to match this picturesque ideal, as nature and art imitated each other. The development of gardens became domesticated with the rage for the picturesque cottage. Humphrey Repton, author of *Fragments and Hints on the Theory and Practice of Landscape Gardening* (1816), advocated the return of the flower garden and the terrace near the house. He suggested using conical trees with classical houses and round headed trees with Gothic buildings to show each off to best advantage (Cat. 70). This gardening style was appropriate for an eclectic age, because it could be adapted to the various types of houses built, ranging from the Italianate and Greek villa to the Gothic or castellated mansion. Conservatories such as those seen in the drawing by George Shepherd (Cat. 87) and the painting of *Tiptree Hall Farm* (Cat. 43) became popular and are evidence of a renewed interest in the cultivation of exotic plants and trees. Above all, the triumph of Repton's approach led the way, on the one hand, to the public park of England, with gardens for everyone and, on the other hand, to the current passion for domestic gardening.

This exhibition may, it is hoped, not only provide a basic survey of the English house and garden from the seventeenth through the nineteenth centuries, but also show how the artist viewed this phenomenon of British society and interpreted it with various methods and materials. That there exist so many examples of house portraiture in art is proof of the integral part the country house played in the history of British life and culture.

Bibliographical References

General reference sources for the histories of the houses, their architects, and owners may be found in:

[George E. Cokayne], *The Complete Peerage,* 13 vols. (London, 1910–59).

Howard M. Colvin, *A Biographical Dictionary of British Architects, 1600-1840* (London, 1978).

John Harris, *A Country House Index* (Shalfleet Manor, 1971, 2nd edition, 1979).

John Summerson, *Architecture in Britain, 1530-1830* (London, 1953).

Other invaluable research sources are articles from *Country Life,* referred to in the *Country Life Index,* and Nikolaus Pevsner's series on *The Buildings of England.*

After this catalogue went to press, John Harris's most detailed survey, *The Artist and the Country House,* London, 1979, appeared. It was too late for extensive use to be made of it but wherever possible, useful information has been extracted and incorporated in the catalogue.

Abbreviations

Brownell 1978	Morris K. Brownell, *Alexander Pope and the Arts of Georgian England*, Oxford, 1978.
Conn	*Connoisseur*
Cornforth 1973	John Cornforth, "Hampton Court, Herefordshire-II," *Country Life* 153 (March 1, 1973): 518-21.
CL	*Country Life*
DNB	*Dictionary of National Biography*, eds. Leslie Stephen and Sidney Lee, 22 vols., London, 1908-1909.
Downes 1966	Kerry Downes, *English Baroque Architecture*, London, 1966.
Egerton	Judy Egerton, *Sporting Art and Books, The Paul Mellon Collection, British Sporting and Animal Paintings*, London, forthcoming.
Guinness and Ryan 1971	Desmond Guinness and William Ryan, *Irish Houses and Castles*, New York, 1971.
Harris 1973	John Harris, *Hampton Court, Herefordshire, 1699-1840*, Sabin Galleries, London, 1973.
Harris 1978	__________"Bird's-Eye Views at Yale," *Country Life* 163 (November 30, 1978): 1820-23.
Harris 1979	__________, *The Artist and the Country House*, London, 1979.
Hill and Cornforth 1966	Oliver Hill and John Cornforth, *English Country Houses, 1625-1685*, London, 1966.
Mack 1969	Maynard Mack, *The Garden and the City: Politics and Retirement in the later Poetry of Pope, 1731-43*, Toronto, 1969.

Praz 1971 | Mario Praz, *Conversation Pieces: A Survey of the Informal Group Portrait in Europe and America*, University Park, 1971.

R.A. | Royal Academician

R.A. 1964-65 | London, Royal Academy, *Painting in England, 1700-1850, from the Collection of Mr. and Mrs. Paul Mellon*, 1964-65.

R.H.A. | Royal Hibernian Academy

Vertue | George Vertue, "Notebooks," 6 vols., *Walpole Society*, 1934-55.

V. & A. | London, Victoria and Albert Museum, *The Garden*, 1979.

V.M.F.A. 1963 | Richmond, Virginia Museum of Fine Arts, *Painting in England, 1700-1850, from the Collection of Mr. and Mrs. Paul Mellon*, 1963.

Walker 1969 | John Walker, "The Thames through 18th-Century Eyes; Augustine Heckell and his Imitators," *Country Life* 146 (July 3, 1969): 24-27.

Yale 1965 | New Haven, Yale University Art Gallery, *Painting in England, 1700-1850, from the Collection of Mr. and Mrs. Paul Mellon*, 1965.

Y.C.B.A. 1977 | New Haven, Yale Center for British Art, *The Pursuit of Happiness*, 1977.

Y.C.B.A., *Selected Paintings*, 1977 | __________, *Selected Paintings, Drawings, and Books*, 1977.

Catalogue

Paintings

1. British School, XVII Century
A VIEW OF LLANNERCH, DENBIGHSHIRE, ca. 1662–72

Oil on canvas, 44 x 59 (111.75 x 150)
B1976.7.115
Coll: Mrs. Patrick Hardman 1967; with Leggatt Brothers from whom pur-
chased 1968
Exh: V. & A. 1979
Lit: Harris 1978, p. 1820, repr. Pl. 1; Harris 1979, (Cat. 41).

When acquired, the painting was described as showing
Massey's Court and a distant view of Wrexham. This is incorrect. The
distant church is the cathedral of St. Asaph, and it is not clear to what
Massey's Court refers. One of the earliest bird's-eye view house
portraits in the collection, the painting shows the house in elevation
while the garden and surrounding countryside are shown naively in
flat plan as viewed from above. Llannerch, on the River Clwyd,
shown in the foreground, is located about twenty-five miles from the
town of Wrexham in northeastern Wales and was owned by the
Griffith family during the sixteenth century. It was passed to Sir Peter
Mutton (ca. 1562-1637), a notable lawyer who became Chief Justice
for North Wales. He built the large grey house seen in this painting
and possibly added to the Griffith house which may be the small red
brick building. The difference in scale between the two buildings is
remarkable. It is a three story "H" plan house with triangular Dutch
style gables. In plan and in the details, such as the triangular gables and
projecting bays on the ends, it compares with Doddington Hall,
Lincolnshire, ca. 1595, and Condover Hall, Shropshire, finished in
1598.

Sir Peter's grandson was Mutton Davies (1633-1684), who
went on the Grand Tour in 1654. He visited the major European
countries and saw elaborate houses and gardens in France and Italy.
On his return to England, and after the Restoration of Charles II, he
seems to have undertaken the creation of the garden at Llannerch
(letter from David Davies-Cook February 6, 1979). Italian gardens
such as those of the Medici at Monte Pincio and the Farnese on the

Palatine Hill may have provided inspiration. These gardens were engraved by Giovanni Battista Falda (1648-1678) in magnificient bird's-eye views which Davies may have seen or even brought back with him. The idea of terracing a steep hill probably came from Italian designs. At Llannerch, broad terraces are constructed on levels punctuated by pavilions, fountains, and summerhouses in a classical style leading down to a circular fountain with Neptune in the center. The terrace idea was not new to England. Wimbleton House, begun 1588, was an actual example, and it was further suggested by William Lawson in his treatise *A New Orchard and Garden* (1618), which included a design for a three-tiered garden with stairways leading from one level to another. The Llannerch garden was described by Philip Yorke in *The Royal Tribes of Wales* published in 1799:

> "The old gardens at Llannerch are within my memory;
> they were made by Mutton Davies in the foreign taste,
> with images and water tricks. Among the rest you were led
> to a sun-dial, which as you approached, spouted
> in your face; on it was written;
> Alas! my friend, time soon will overtake you;
> And if you do not cry, by G-d I'll make you."

The sundial at the top left cannot be the one referred to. There is a larger version of the painting showing the same view in the possession of the Davies family at their house in Gwysaney, Wales. It is inscribed in a seventeenth-century hand "The Prospect of Llannerch taken on the East Side, 1662," which is the source for our dating of the painting. It may be that 1662 was the date the work commenced, so that a date of ca. 1662-72 is preferred for the painting.

2.   Jan Siberechts (1627–ca. 1700)
A VIEW OF BAYHALL, PEMBURY, KENT, ca. 1675–85

Oil on canvas, 45 x 69 (114.5 x 175.5)
No. 989
Coll: Thornton-Smith; with Sabin Galleries from whom purchased 1963
Lit: Hill and Cornforth 1966, p. 222, repr. Fig. 375; Egerton (Cat. 4); Harris
      1979 (Cat. 68).

This bird's-eye view represents the variety of human activities which can take place in the complex society of the country house: hunting, boating, coaching and promenading in the formal landscaped area.

The house and land were granted to Richard Amherst, Serjeant-at-Law, by James I in the early seventeenth century. The house was rebuilt by his son Richard Amherst during Cromwell's Protectorate and was completed around 1664. As shown in the painting, it was a three-story building with a front facade delineated by eight giant pilasters. The hipped roof was penetrated by dormer windows capped with triangular pediments. Six tall brick chimneys crowned the massive square house. The building was demolished in 1908.

There is a smaller version of the painting in Tryon Palace, New Bern, North Carolina. There is said to be the central fragment of another view at Amherst College, but its present location is unknown. The existence of several different versions is not unusual with topographical view painting in England.

Siberechts was born in Antwerp and came to England between 1672 and 1674. He changed his style and became a specialist in portraits of country houses, including Longleat, Chatsworth and Wollaton (see Cat. 3). This example may have been painted soon after his arrival in England when he had to learn a new technique suitable for topography. In it, Siberechts's use of perspective is less sophisticated than in his view of Wollaton, and can be compared to that of Longleat (ca. 1675). Taking into account other works by Siberechts as well as the costume of the woman at the left, a date of about 1675–85 is proposed for this painting.

3. Jan Siberechts (1627–ca. 1700)
WOLLATON HALL AND PARK, NOTTINGHAMSHIRE, 1697

Signed, *J. Siberechts 1697,* lower left
Oil on canvas, 75½ x 54½ (191.8 x 138.4)
B1973.1.52
Coll: Sir Thomas Willoughby; Mrs. H. L. Birkin (a descendant by marriage
    of Sir Francis Willoughby); sold Sotheby's July 11, 1962 (18); with
    P.& D. Colnaghi from whom purchased 1962
Exh: V.M.F.A. 1963 (5), repr. Pl. 168; R.A. 1964–65 (300), repr. Pl. 75;
    Y.C.B.A. 1977 (136); V. & A. 1979
Lit: Harris 1978, repr. Pl. 2; Harris 1979 (Cat. 70).

Wollaton Hall, located near Nottingham, was built for Sir
Francis Willoughby in 1580–88. As the Sheriff of Nottinghamshire,
Sir Francis had entertained Queen Elizabeth I during one of her
summer progresses and, perhaps in anticipation of another visit,
sought to create an even grander palace to receive her. The house was
probably designed by Robert Smythson (ca. 1536–1614), a professional English architect trained under Sir John Thynne at Longleat
House. Smythson incorporated and adapted details and motifs from
the architectural pattern books of Sebastiano Serlio (1475–1552),
which were published in English from 1516 onwards, as well as
those of the Fleming, Vredeman de Vries (1527–after 1604).

The house, as depicted in the painting and as it was built, was
revolutionary in plan because it was based on an "E" shape rather
than the traditional enclosed courtyard plan. It is outward looking,
with many large windows and without the confining interior courtyard. The square mass of house is topped by an enormous banqueting hall used for dining, for gazing over the grounds, or for watching
the course of a hunt. The exterior is covered with Netherlandish
ornament, strapwork gables and banded pilasters, all derived from
de Vries's pattern book. Wollaton Hall is now owned by the City of
Nottingham and is the local natural history museum.

The garden, as shown, dates from the seventeenth century
and is characterized by parterres, geometric plantings and *allées* of
trees. These formal elements came to England from Italy indirectly
by way of France and the Netherlands. The central fountain, with
water rising from the circumference, may have been designed by
Smythson. Beyond the formal garden with its regularly planted
trees and avenues are the kitchen gardens where vegetables and herbs
are grown and clothes laid out to dry. The long one-story building in

the foreground may be an orangery or greenhouse, where trees were cultivated in tubs to be placed outdoors in the warm seasons. A small banqueting house overlooks the broad bowling lawn at the side of the house. Throughout the painting, the artist depicts small details of daily life at a country house.

The painting was commissioned by Sir Thomas Willoughby, Bart. (ca. 1670–1729), later 1st Lord Middleton. Another version, dated 1695, by the same artist shows the house in a horizontal composition with the gardens extended to the left (Lord Middleton Collection, Birdsall House, Yorkshire).

4. Leonard Knyff(1650–1722)
THE NORTH PROSPECT OF HAMPTON COURT, HEREFORDSHIRE, WITH PARK AND DECOY, 1699

Signed, *L. Knyff 1699,* lower center
Inscribed, *The north Prospect of/ Hampton Court with ye/ Park and Decoy by
        Mr. Knife,* lower right
Oil on canvas 58⅜ x 84⅜ (148.5 x 214.5)
No. 1989
Coll: Painted for Thomas, Lord Coningsby; Margaret Countess of
        Coningsby; by descent to Viscount Malden, later 5th Earl of Essex;
        Richard Arkwright, Esq., who acquired Hampton Court in 1810;
        Mrs. Burrell, who acquired Hampton Court in 1912; Viscountess
        Hereford; with Sabin Galleries from whom purchased 1972
Lit: Harris 1973 (Cat. 1) repr. front cover and Pl. 7; Cornforth 1973, p. 518,
        repr. Pl 2; Harris 1979 (Cat. 115b).

Sir Rowland Lenthall was granted a license by the king to erect a fortified structure in 1434, and in the same year built Hampton Court. This picture shows most of the original crenellated manor with four ranges around a central court. A large ornamental decoy is shown in the foreground. The house and land were later sold to the Coningsby family. A brick addition to the south side of the house, more clearly seen in the companion picture also by Knyff (Cat. 5), was built in the 1680s by Thomas Coningsby, later Lord Coningsby. He soon came to regret this modern addition, as he developed an intense interest in medieval history and his Coningsby ancestors. Both paintings represent the house before his later alterations. A view of the north facade of Hampton Court as altered by Coningsby between 1706 and 1710 to a more symmetrical medieval appearance is in the background of his portrait by Thomas Bate

(Ulster Museum, Belfast), where he is shown, incidentally, in classical dress with a cuirass, lance and quiver of arrows. Engravings of Hampton Court, Herefordshire, published in *Vitruvius Britannicus* (1717) document this change. These alterations were perhaps executed from the designs of William Talman, retaining the crenellated style of the original house but imposing a more regular order on the design (Cornforth 1973, p. 520).

The house was again remodelled between 1791 and 1795. This time, a gothic style was used for Lord Malden, who had acquired the house in 1781. These alterations can be seen in the two watercolors by Turner (Cats. 78 and 79). It was further gothicized in the 1830s and early 1840s by Charles Hanbury-Tracey and John Atkinson for John Arkwright, whose family had bought the house sometime between 1808 and 1810. Until recently it belonged to Lord Hereford.

This and the following two further views of Hampton Court (Cats. 5 and 6) show the range of activities that might occur in the vicinity of a country house: hawking, fox hunting, shooting, bowling, coaching, haymaking, poultry feeding, cow milking and sailing, with the Rivers Lugg and Arrow used for barges.

Leonard Knyff was born in Haarlem, where his father Wouter Knyff was a painter. The young Knyff went to England in 1681 where he worked, apart from occasional visits to Holland, for the rest of his life. He is best known for his bird's-eye views of English country houses engraved by Johannes Kip. The engravings appeared in 1707 and subsequently with additions in folio volumes entitled *Britannia Illustrata* (Cat. 97).

5. Leonard Knyff (1650-1722)
THE SOUTHEAST PROSPECT OF HAMPTON COURT, HEREFORDSHIRE, ca. 1699

Signed, *L. Knyff,* lower right
Inscribed, *The South East Prospect/ of Hampton Court in-/ Herifordsheir/ by L. Kniff,* lower right
Oil on canvas, 58½ x 84⅜ (148.5 x 214.5)
No. 1930
Coll: See Cat. 4
Lit: Harris 1973 (Cat. 2), repr. back cover; Harris 1978, repr. Pl. 3; Cornforth 1973, p. 520, repr. Pl. 7; Harris 1979 (Cat. 115a).

This picture, as in the following view by Stevens (Cat. 6), shows Lord Coningsby's alterations, dated to about 1680, to the south front of Hampton Court with a two-story, three-bay addition of brick with a hipped roof. The large garden is defined by *allées* of trees and parterres in the French manner. George London, the celebrated garden-designer, seems to have been responsible for the design of the garden at the time this painting was begun. He worked under the supervision of William Talman, who may have designed the unusual cruciform temple seen at the termination of the long path to the right. The painting may record the ending of one phase of work before the fountain seen in the following painting was introduced.

Water in large flat pools and canals was an important part of the English seventeenth-century garden. William Lawson described its many uses in *A New Orchard and Garden:*

> "Water would offer you fish, fence, and moisture to your trees, and pleasure also. . . You may have swans and other water birds, good for devouring vermin, and a boat for many good uses."

6. John Stevens (d. 1722)
SOUTH PROSPECT OF HAMPTON COURT, HEREFORD-
SHIRE, ca. 1706-10

Inscribed, *The South/ Prospect of-/ Hampton Court/ in Herifordsheir/ Don by
      Mr. Stevens,* lower left
Oil on canvas, 82 x 94 (207.6 x 238.1)
No. 1960
Coll: Same as *North Prospect of Hampton Court* (Cat. 4); with Christopher
      Gibbs from whom purchased 1972
Lit: John Steegman, *The Artist and the Country House* (London, 1949), p. 24,
      repr. Fig. 2; John Cornforth, "Hampton Court, Herefordshire—I"
      CL 153 (February 22, 1973): 451, repr. Pl. 4; Harris 1973 (Cat. 3);
      Harris 1978, repr. Pl. 4; Harris 1979 (Cat. 120).

This bird's-eye view is more naive and maplike than the two Knyff paintings of the same subject (Cats. 4 and 5). All three views were commissioned by Lord Coningsby and reflect his pride and interest in the house and its environs.

This picture shows the house as altered by Lord Coningsby in the late 1680s but not as altered by him about 1710. Here, the north range still includes the chimneys that no longer appear in engravings of the house published in *Vitruvius Britannicus* in 1717. The gate tower faces the entrance to the great hall, where two windows flank the chimney stack in the center of the south range. To the east lie the old private apartments refaced as a two-story building of five bays. To the west is a projecting block of three bays dating from the 1680s.

The extensive formal gardens of Hampton Court are clearly seen in this view. This planting must post-date the *Southeast Prospect* by Knyff (Cat. 5), because it includes the large Neptune fountain in the foreground described by Tom Lyttleton in 1758 in a letter to Mrs. Montagu:

> "In the middle [of the garden] is a piece of water of about an acre, cut into two square lines, in which, to the astonishment of the beholder, you see Neptune upon his throne, and twenty Tritons waiting behind him. The carver has express'd great fierceness in his countenance and well may the god, who shakes the earth with his Trident, be angry at being confined to a Pool which would scarce hold two hundred fish."

The addition of the fountain is the most significant difference from the two previous views by Knyff. According to Harris, it could be compared to that designed for the forecourt of Buckingham House, ca. 1705. Because of the dated drawings cited by Cornforth, which show no alterations in 1706, a date of ca. 1706-10 is suggested for this view by the mysterious Mr. Stevens, about whom little is known, apart from the exact date of his death.

7. British School, XVII Century
A PERSPECTIVE VIEW OF DENHAM PLACE, BUCKING-
HAMSHIRE, ca. 1695

Oil on canvas, 40 x 49¾ (101.6 x 126.4)
B1976.7.116
Coll: Probably commissioned by Sir Roger Hill, Denham Place; by family
    descent to Mrs. Lewis Way; by descent in the Way family until 1920
    when Denham Place was sold to Mr. and Mrs. Fothergill; acquired
    by Lord Vansittart in 1930; Lady Vansittart; sold Sotheby's,
    December 18, 1968 (210) as by Danckerts; bt. Sabin Galleries from
    whom purchased 1968
Exh: V. & A. 1979
Lit: Christopher Hussey, "Denham Place-I-Buckinghamshire, The Seat of
    Mr. and Mrs. Basil Fothergill," *CL* 57 (April 18, 1925): 608, repr.
    Fig. 14; John Harris, "The Building of Denham Place," *Journal of the
    Buckinghamshire Archaeological Society* (1957), p. 193, repr. Pl. XII;
    Hill and Cornforth 1966, repr. Fig. 343; Harris 1979 (Cat. 121).

26

This bird's-eye view shows the large impressive house built for Sir Roger Hill between 1688 and 1701. Sir Roger served as High Sheriff of Buckinghamshire in 1673. In that year, he bought the west half of the estate at Denham, but did not start building until 1688. The house was erected as an H-shaped, two-story structure, with a hipped roof and an eleven bay facade. The stable block with cupolas probably dates from the same period. (Hussey, p. 602). The house remained in the Hill family until 1905. It underwent many alterations; the roof balustrade and tall cupola have now disappeared, but it remains a private house.

The gardens existed almost exactly as shown in the painting. There was a formal flat layout with canals, topiary, trellis work and sculpture. The popularity of garden sculpture derived from the Netherlands; it came into vogue when William and Mary came to the English throne in 1688. William Stanton, as architect and sculptor, was probably responsible for some of the figures at Denham. Richard Osgood, according to the account books of Sir Roger Hill, was paid forty pounds on March 3, 1694, for "figures upon the Great Gates" (Harris, p. 194). These figures are perhaps Gog and Magog, ancient gods who, in British legend, were the sole survivors of a family of monstrous creatures slain by demons. There were thirty-four sculpted dancing boys on the long wall, and fragments of these still exist.

Through the garden from east to west ran the Misbourne River which had been made into a canal for Sir Roger Hill. The pavilion that appears to be standing in the canal may have been a remnant from an earlier house on the site. It is supported on arches above the water, and served as a gazebo from which to view the scenery. The formal garden was demolished and "improved" in 1771 by Lancelot "Capability" Brown.

8.   Leonard Knyff (1650-1722)
BLACK GAME, RABBITS AND SWALLOWS IN THE PARK OF A COUNTRY HOUSE, ca. 1700

Signed, *L. Knyff,* on rock, lower left
Oil on canvas, 35½ x 56 (90 x 142)
B1973.1.44
Coll: Col. John Alston, London; sold by his executors, Christie's, June 20, 1969 (112); bt. Baskett from whom purchased 1969
Exh: Y.C.B.A., *Wildlife in British Art,* 1978

Lit: "Notes and Queries," *Conn*, 98 (November 1936); 299, with an enquiry, signed "L.B.," about the identity of the house; Y.C.B.A., *Selected Paintings*, p. 7; Egerton (Cat. 8); Harris 1979 (Cat. 103).

Knyff is best known for his meticulous renderings of country houses, such as the two paintings of Hampton Court, Herefordshire, in this exhibition (Cats. 4 and 5). The manor house in the background may have actually existed, and its owner may have commissioned the scene, but for the present, the identity of the house is unknown. It was probably not built as a fortified castle because of the large size of the windows in the corner towers. These are similar in structure and fenestration to those at Longford Castle, near Salisbury, Wiltshire, which was built in 1591. Longford, however, was designed in a triangular plan and was never crenellated, as is this house.

Knyff painted a variety of subjects including still-lifes and sporting scenes, as well as animals and game birds. Those in the foreground here represent black grouse: two cocks and a gray hen.

9. British School XVIII Century
THE EARL OF ROCHESTER'S HOUSE, NEW PARK, RICHMOND, SURREY, ca. 1700–1705

Oil on canvas, 42¼ x 83½ (107.2) x 212)
No. 1740
Coll: With David Stockwell, Wilmington, Delaware, from whom
    purchased 1971
Lit: Harris 1978, repr. Pl. 6; Harris 1979 (Cat. 154).

This area of the Thames Valley, just above Twickenham, is one of the most painted riverscapes in Britain. The vicinity was popular among country house owners, as it was only two hours on horseback from Hyde Park and the heart of London. James Thomson described the area in 1765: "Heavens! What a goodly prospect spreads around, of hills and dales and woods and lawns and spires, and glittering towns and gilded streams withall" (Brian Dunning, "The Changing Thames at Richmond," *CL*, 143 [January 25, 1968] :164).

The identity of this house is not known for certain, but is probably Petersham Lodge, which was also called Richmond New Park. The park itself had been enclosed by Charles I in 1637 and given to the people of London in 1650. After the Restoration of

Charles II, it was given back to the king by the populace. In 1686, the plot of land and the house built on it at the northeast corner of the park was given by James II to his nephew, Viscount Cornbury (1661-1723), who either sold or transferred it to his cousin, Laurence Hyde (1642-1711), who was created 1st Earl of Rochester in 1686. In 1692-93 Lord Rochester contracted with Matthew Banckes (d. 1706) to rebuild the house on the property. In 1711, the estate passed to his son, the 2nd Earl of Rochester. It burned down in 1721, and was rebuilt by William, Earl of Harrington around 1742.

An engraving of the house and its extensive formal gardens, included in Kip and Knyff's *Britannia Illustrata* (1707), is inscribed "New Parce in Surrey, the Seat of the Rt. Honble the Earle of Rochester." It shows vast formal gardens in the French style with parterres, *allées,* and geometric plantings. These gardens with several fountains appear faintly in the painting to the left of the house. Outbuildings included a brewhouse and a dovecote (probably the tower-like structure to the right of the main house). The buildings with large windows may have been orangeries or tennis courts. The small building in the right foreground may be a pottery.

It has been suggested by Harris that the artist may be Adrian van Diest (1655/56-1704) a Dutchman who came to England at the age of seventeen in 1672. A prolific artist, he painted hundreds of idealized landscapes in the manner of Claude and Poussin. Van Diest painted at least one country seat, Dunham Massey, Cheshire, in 1696 (National Trust, Dunham Massey). He was employed around 1700 at Ham House near Richmond New Park to paint overmantel and overdoor scenes, and the Earl of Rochester may have commissioned him to execute this picture for nearby Petersham Lodge.

10. British School XVIII Century
BIFRONS PARK, KENT, ca. 1705-10

Oil on canvas, 61½ x 91½ (86.8 x 132.5)
B1977.14.83
Coll: Samuel Courtauld; Lord Butler, K.G.; with Thos. Agnew & Sons
     from whom purchased 1977 as by J. Wootton
Lit: Harris 1978, p. 1823, repr. Pl. 7; Harris 1979 (Cat. 73) as attributed to Jan
     Siberechts.

This painting shows the transition from the bird's-eye view to the man's-eye view. The artist stands on a hill above the house and looks down toward it. Bifrons House does not dominate, but is part of the landscape which includes the tall tower of Canterbury Cathedral on the left.

The house was originally built by John Bargrave who died in 1600. It was called Bifrons because of the "bi-front" arrangement of two projecting bays in a modified "E" plan. It was acquired by John Taylor in 1694 and remained in the Taylor family throughout the eighteenth century. The most renowned member of the family was Dr. Brook Taylor, the author of two important books on perspective which were widely used by artists. The house was demolished in 1948.

The painting was formerly attributed to John Wootton (?1686-1764) and was thought to have been an early landscape executed under the influence of his Dutch teacher, Jan Wyck. Wootton's earliest known works date around 1718 when he was about twenty-two, and the costume of the figures in the foreground of this painting cannot be much later than 1705-10. This seems to rule out Wootton as the artist. The treatment of the landscape painting is also more precise than Wootton's style. Jan Siberechts has also been considered as a possible artist, but there is insufficient evidence for this attribution, as a comparison with Cats. 2 and 3 shows. It has also been suggested that perhaps the figures are by a different hand. The painting does show an early and fresh view of the English landscape with effects of light and atmosphere in the Kent countryside. The artist may indeed have been Netherlandish.

The garden is a more intimate and less contrived space than earlier examples in this exhibition (such as *Hampton Court* and *Denham Place*, Cats. 5, 6 and 7), and appears to represent an early trend toward a less rigidly constructed landscape mode.

11. British School XVIII Century
PROSPECT OF THE PIERREPONT HOUSE, NOTTING-
HAM, ca. 1708-13.

Oil on canvas, 36 x 48 (91.5 x 122)
B1976.7.125
Coll: Major A. W. Foster, Apley Park, Bridgenorth, Salop; sold Christie's
    July 3, 1964 (59) as by Leonard Knyff; bt. Sabin Galleries from whom
    purchased 1966
Exh: Y.C.B.A. 1977 (137); V. & A. 1979
Lit: Harris 1979 (Cat. 109).

This town house was built by Francis Pierrepont, third son of Robert, Earl of Kingston, before 1654 when John Evelyn wrote that he had seen the house during his travels. The tower of Saint Mary's Church which was adjacent to the Pierrepont House stands at the left. Both the church and the house appear almost exactly the same in Leonard Knyff's view of Nottingham from the east, engraved by Johannes Kip for *Le Nouveau Théâtre de la Grande Bretagne* (London, 1708). The smaller house, however, which can be seen in the painting between the church and Pierrepont House, does not appear in the engraving. This may be Plumptre House. Pierrepont House is no longer standing, and the garden was demolished in 1800 when a street was put in its place (letter from A.J.N. Henstock, County Archivist, Notts., Oct. 24, 1972).

The sunken formal garden was laid out after 1677, because it does not appear in the engraved view of the site published in Dr. Robert Thornton's *Antiquities of Nottingham,* 1677. This is a typical, small enclosed garden influenced by French and Dutch designs. It consists of a parterre near the house, ornamented with geometric beds, called knots or trails, with a walk bordered with hedges and trees that were kept closely clipped. The use of flower pots is documented and advocated by John Worlidge in *Systema Horticultura* (1677), a popular instructive garden book:

> "Other ancient ornaments for a garden are Flower-Pots, which painted white and placed on pedestals, either on the ground in a straight line on the edges of your walks, or at the corners of your Squares, are exceeding pleasant . . . They are usually made of Potter's Clay; But to prevent that casualty of breaking, some are made of lead which are much to be preferred."

The painting was formerly attributed to Leonard Knyff, but comparison to documented Knyff works, such as *Hampton Court, Herefordshire* (see Cats. 4 and 5) makes this attribution doubtful. The picture seems to have been painted in the first decade of the eighteenth century (judging from the costume), when the house was owned by the Hon. William Pierrepont (1692-1713).

12. Matthias Read (1669–1747)
PROSPECT VIEW OF WHITEHAVEN, CUMBRIA, SHOW-
ING FLATT HALL, TO THE LEFT ca. 1730–35

Oil on canvas, 40 x 72 (101.6 x 183)
No. 3075
Coll: Commissioned by the Lowther family for Flatt Hall; with Sir William
     Lowther, Holker Hall, by 1756; by descent to the Rt. Hon. the Earl
     of Lonsdale; sold Sotheby's, November 27, 1974 (49); bt. John
     Baskett from whom acquired 1974
Lit: William Jackson, *Papers and Pedigrees Mainly Relating to Cumberland and
     Westmoreland*, 2 vols. (London, 1892), 1:93; Harris 1979 (Cat. 167).

According to Daniel Hay of Whitehaven (cited in the Sotheby
catalogue, 1974), Read's view must have been painted between 1730
and 1735: after the lighthouse on Old Quay was moved and before
Merchant's Tongue Quay was completed. Read probably painted a
later version of the scene, since an engraving by Richard Parr (1738)
after a view by Read incorporates several features of the town and
harbor not represented in this painting (*Victoria History of the Counties
of England; Cumberland*, 2 vols.- [London, 1905-], 2: repr. p. 362).
The present scene is recorded in the will of Sir William Lowther (d.
1756), as *A Prospect of Whitehaven from Brackenthwaite about 1730*.

Read's bird's-eye view of Whitehaven, on the northwest
coast of England, shows the nearby seat of the Lowther family on the
eastern edge of town (left). One of the earliest post-medieval
planned towns in England, Whitehaven was developed under the
direction of Sir John Lowther (1642–1705), who transformed the
small fishing village (there had been around nine thatched cottages in
1633) into an important coal center. Sir John acquired land grants
from Charles II, expanded mines outside the town, improved roads
and expanded the harbor so that by the end of the seventeenth
century it was capable of holding 100 sailing ships.

As the painting shows, Whitehaven was laid out in a simple
grid plan, with one block left free for St. Nicholas Church (center).
This was placed on its site with some care, since Sir John "was very
desirous to lay out a street from his private gate, down which the
harbour might be visible," and did not want the church to block his
view (Jackson, *Cumberland*, 1: 229). Jackson's history of Whitehaven
also includes an old map which clearly shows the long street from the
"Flatt" or "Flatt Hall" as the house was called, straight to the water's
edge. Described in 1680 as a "stately new pile of a building," Sir

John's house was erected on the site of an old manor called "The Castle" (William Whelan, *History of . . . Cumberland,* London, 1860, p. 440). Sir John's son, Sir James Lowther (?1673-1755), inherited Flatt Hall and continued the development his father had begun in opening up new coal mines and expanding the port until it became second or third in importance in England. The next to inherit Flatt Hall was Sir John Lowther, who made extensive alterations and additions to the original house in 1769, and re-named it The Castle. It is now part of the Whitehaven Hospital.

Jackson's history also includes a brief biographical sketch of Read (1: 89-93) which notes that he began his career as a native of Whitehaven "daubing colours on heads and sterns of ships," and was later patronized by William Gilpin, grandfather of the Rev. William Gilpin, the writer on the picturesque. Read painted local landscapes, portraits and history subjects and "there was hardly a house in Whitehaven, whose master could afford it, which had not a picture or two painted in panels over doors or chimneys by his hand."

13. Charles Philips (1708-1747)
THE FINCH FAMILY, ca. 1731-32

Signed, *CPhilips pinxit.,* lower left
Oil on canvas, 39½ x 49½ (100.4 x 125.7)
No. 625
Coll: By descent from Lady Isabella Finch (on the far right in the portrait), who brought the picture to her house at 44 Berkeley Square, London; bequeathed to her niece, Lady Anne Wentworth, Countess Fitzwilliam (standing center); by descent in the Fitzwilliam family, Wentworth Woodhouse, Yorkshire until 1949; with Gooden & Fox from whom purchased 1963
Exh: Leeds City Art Gallery, *Treasures from Yorkshire House,* 1950 (41), repr.; V.M.F.A. 1963 (218) repr.

The thirteen figures in this complex conversation piece are the two sons, four daughters, one son-in-law and five grandchildren (with a nurse) of Daniel Finch (1647-1730), 2nd Earl of Nottingham, 7th Earl of Winchelsea, by his second wife Anne, daughter of Christopher, Viscount Hatton. Their unusually grandiose background is thought to be a commentary on fashionable architectural taste of the 1730s, which would be particularly apt as one member of the group was then engaged in building Wentworth Woodhouse, one of the largest houses in England.

Thomas Watson Wentworth (1693-1750), Baron Malton and later 1st Marquess of Rockingham, is the man on the far right in the picture who gestures toward his wife, Mary Finch, with one of her brothers and her five children in the center of the composition. Early in the 1720s, Lord Malton had begun to rebuild his family seat at Wentworth Woodhouse, Yorkshire, probably from the plans of James Gibbs. By the early 1730s, Lord Burlington's influence in Yorkshire had become pervasive and Lord Malton abandoned his earlier plan to adopt a new one by Henry Flitcroft, who designed an east front 660 feet long in a pure Palladian style. Although work did not begin until 1734, several years after this painting, Lord Malton was probably already involved in the change from an ornate baroque to a simplified classical plan. When the painting was exhibited at Leeds in 1950, the unidentified compiler of the pamphlet suggested that Philips may have symbolized Malton's new taste by opposing two triumphal arches in the background in the Finch painting. The one on the right:

> "bathed in the warm glow of the rising sun, its simple candid lines and harmonious proportions . . . [is] clearly juxtaposed to the ponderous Roman triumphal arch with its crumbling overgrown attic and baroque accretions standing dark, ghostly and forgotten on the left."

The artist also refers to Lord Malton's taste in landscape design by his prominent placement of an obelisk, a favored garden ornament of Burlington and Pope, between the two structures.

An unsigned replica of this painting which descended in the family of the Earls Fitzwilliam at Wentworth Woodhouse, is now in the family possession at Milton, Peterbourgh.

14. British School XVIII Century
CALKE ABBEY, DERBYSHIRE, ca. 1734

Oil on canvas, 23¾ x 35¾ (60.3 x 90.6)
B1976.7.117
Coll: Probably commissioned by Sir John Harpur, 4th Bart., who built Calke Abbey; by descent to his daughter Jemima Harpur, who married Sir Thomas Palmer, 4th Bart. (d. 1765); by descent in the Palmer family; with Sabin Galleries from whom purchased 1969
Lit: Downes 1966, repr. Pl. 382; Harris 1979 (Cat. 144).

The painting of the house fills the breadth of the canvas almost to the edges of the frame in a composition similar to an architect's rendering. The foreground figures were added after Calke was painted, as may be noted in the pentimenti of the steps showing through their bodies. They are probably members of the family of Sir John Harpur, 4th Bart. (1679-1741), who employed Francis Smith of Warwick (1672-1738) in 1703 as his architect to commence the building of Calke. The noted architect, James Gibbs (1682-1754) designed the balustraded flight of steps up to the main entrance. These were removed after 1790 when a new Ionic portico was added to the facade, and the six Corinthian capitals on the pilasters were altered to match. The house is still extant.

The painting is thought to date from around the time of the marriage in 1734 of Sir John Harpur's eldest son and heir, Sir Henry Harpur (?1708-48) to Lady Caroline Manners. The heraldic device on the panel of the carriage shows that the coat of arms of the Harpurs and Manners are joined, or "impaled." Supporting this date are the costumes, which appear to date in the mid-1730s.

15. Arthur Devis (1712-1787), and an Unknown Artist, possibly James Seymour (1702-1752)
LEAK OKEOVER, REV. JOHN ALLEN, AND CAPT. CHESTER IN THE GROUNDS OF OKEOVER HALL, STAFFORDSHIRE, 1745-47

Oil on canvas, 38½ x 48½ (97.7 x 123.2)
No. 239
Coll: Commissioned by Leak Okeover for Okeover Hall; Sir Walter Gilbey; sold Christie's, March 12, 1910 (142) as *Portrait of the Grey Horse "Palfy" with a Groom in a Landscape,* as by Seymour and Zoffany; bt. Leggatt Brothers; 5th Earl of Rosebery (d. 1929), The Durdans, Epsom, Surrey; in 1960, with Partridge, New York, as *Frederick, 2nd Viscount Bolingbroke and his Two Brothers Henry and John, with Mr. Wildman, "Gimcrack," and Groom in the Grounds of Stratton Park, Hampshire,* as attributed to Arthur Devis; acquired in 1960
Exh: V.M.F.A. 1963 (448) as *Portrait Group with Horses and Dog,* as by James Seymour and an unidentified artist
Lit: Arthur Oswald, "Okeover Hall, Staffordshire, II, the Seat of Sir Ian Walker-Okeover, Bt.," *CL* 135 (January 30, 1964): 228, Arthur Oswald, "Conversation Piece in the Making," *CL* 137 (January 21, 1965): 108-109, repr. Fig. 1; Egerton (Cat. 58); Harris 1979 (Cat. 233).

The identification of the sitters and the house in this portrait was first noted by Arthur Oswald from contemporary letters to Leak Okeover (deposited in the Derbyshire Record Office, Matlock). Probably the seated man on the right, Okeover (1701–65) was passionately devoted to the renovation and embellishment of his family country seat, Okeover Hall, an Elizabethan manor house which he inherited in 1729. By 1744, his architect, Joseph Sanderson, embarked on an ambitious building scheme, beginning with the east and west ranges; and in 1746, Sanderson was ready to commence work on the south front, the view shown in Devis's painting. By that time, Devis had already gone to Okeover to make sketches of the house, and Sanderson, having seen the unfinished picture in Devis's studio, wrote to Okeover with a new idea:

> "Mr. Davise [sic] shewd me the S. front of the House as he sketchd it on the spot, Now Sir, please to consider if it shall be drawn in the pickture as it is at present, or according to the new Design I have made, which I believe will be the same to Mr. Davise to paint, or if you would have a Drawing of the new design introduced . . . ."

Okeover assented and Devis duly altered his painting to show the projected temple front with Doric columns *in antis* supporting a pedimented central bay. Sanderson died in 1747, however, and work was delayed until 1751 when Okeover fled his creditors to France, £24,000 in debt. Refusing to sell Okeover Hall—"I will much sooner never see England again than do it," Okeover settled his finances and, in the late 1750s, turned again to rebuilding Okeover Hall under the direction of Simon File, Sanderson's assistant. Most of the original plan was carried out, but Sanderson's portico, shown in Devis's painting, was never executed. With that exception, Devis's view of the house, its chapel and stable wing from a hill side to the south, is an accurate one. The house has undergone further restorations in the nineteenth and twentieth centuries but still remains in the Okeover family possession.

The portrait was commissioned to fit into a panel over a fireplace at Okeover Hall. At some time during its execution, Devis must have called upon another artist, probably Seymour, to paint the horses and dogs. They are uncharacteristic of Devis's more generalized style in painting animals and probably represent, with some fidelity, Okeover's prized horses and pets.

16. Arthur Devis (1712-1787)
ROBERT GWILLYM AND HIS FAMILY AT ATHERTON
HALL, LANCASHIRE, ca. 1745-47

Oil on canvas, 39⅛ x 49⅝ (99.5 x 126)
B1977.14.51
Coll: By family descent to Thomas Powys, 2nd Baron Lilford, who mar-
    ried, in 1797, Henrietta Maria, daughter of Robert Vernon Atherton
    (formerly Gwillym, the boy in the portrait); Lord Lilford, Lilford
    Hall, Northamptonshire, until 1961; with Sabin Galleries from
    whom purchased 1961
Exh: V.M.F.A. 1963 (227), repr. Pl. 84; R.A. 1964-65 (204), repr. on cover;
    Yale 1965 (75), repr. on back cover; in all exhibitions above, identi-
    fied as *Robert Vernon Atherton and his Family;* Y.C.B.A. 1977 (135),
    repr.
Lit: John Baskett, "Painting in England, 1700-1850," *Conn* 153 (June 1963):
    101; "Collector's Questions," *CL* 134 (September 5, 1963): 536,
    repr.; John Cornforth, "The Informality of English Painting," *CL
    Annual* (1965): 18 repr.; Christopher Neve, "Arthur Devis, a Minor
    English Master," *CL Annual* (1972): 44, repr.; Praz 1971, p. 138,
    repr. Pl. 96; above references as *Robert Vernon Atherton and his Family;*
    Harris 1979 (Cat. 231).

Atherton Hall, about five miles southwest of Bolton,
Lancashire, was begun in 1723 by Richard Atherton (d. 1726),
from the designs of William Wakefield, an amateur Yorkshire architect. The unfinished house was inherited by Atherton's daughter
Elizabeth (seated on the right), whose husband Robert Gwillym
(standing second from left) completed the house in 1743 at a cost of
£63,000. The couple are shown here with their four children: Robert
Vernon (1741-83), Jane, Elizabeth and William (d. 1771), and possibly with Gwillym's father and brother. The house was demolished
in 1825.

The accuracy of Devis's rendering is problematical. Atherton
Hall was published in the third volume of Colen Campbell's *Vitruvius
Britannicus,* 1725 (see the glass case display, Cat. 98). The engraving
shows a projected plan and elevation for a 102 foot long front with a
central bay of three windows over three, framed by four engaged
columns surmounted by a pediment, and side bays with two windows
over two. Although Devis's Atherton is similar to this plan in its
high rusticated basement, steps, corner pilasters and central window
construction, the painted version shows no engaged columns and
pediment, and the side bays are reduced to one window over one.

The problem is further complicated by the existence of a print, dated 1823 (John Lunn, *History of Atherton* [Atherton, 1971], repr. p. 54) which represents the house set back into a wooded parkland but otherwise just as it was planned and represented in *Vitruvius Britannicus*. Yet neither print shows the flanking pavillions, one of which survived the demolition of Atherton in 1825 (Downes 1966, Pls. 325-26), which Devis includes in his representation of Atherton. It may be concluded therefore that the later print took its elevation from Campbell's book and that Devis's rendering is accurate. It was probably sketched on the spot, as was his painting of *Okeover Hall* (Cat. 15), and reflects the retrenchment by Gwillym of his father-in-law's grandiose building scheme.

17. Joseph Nickolls (active 1720–ca. 1755), ascribed to
POPE'S VILLA, TWICKENHAM, ca. 1755

Oil on canvas, 17½ x 32 (44.5 x 81.2)
B1976.7.135
Coll: With Spink and Son from whom purchased 1960
Exh: V.M.F.A. 1963 (15); Y.C.B.A. 1977 (138).
Lit: Christopher Hussey, "Twickenham I," *CL* 96 (September 8, 1944): 420-23; Hugh Phillips, *The Thames about 1750* (London 1951) p. 193; Walker 1969, pp. 24-27; Mack 1969; p. 284, repr. Pl. 14; Luke Hermann, *British Landscape Painting of the 18th Century* (London, 1974), p. 34, repr.; Brownell 1978, p. 374.

Alexander Pope (1688-1744), noted author and poet, leased the villa and five acres of land along the Thames in 1719. This area, called Twickenham, near the town of Richmond about ten miles from London, was a fashionable center in the early eighteenth century. Great examples of domestic architecture such as Marble Hill, Mount Lebanon, York House, Orleans House and Strawberry Hill were built here. This area was also the site of some of the first "suburbs" such as Richmond Green, Kew Green and Ham Common. Daniel Defoe remarked in *On a Tour thro' the Whole Island of Great Britain* (1724), about Twickenham:

> "The whole country here shines with a lustre not to be described; take then in a remote view, the fine seats shine among the trees as Jewels shine in a rich Coronet; in a near sight, they are meer Pictures and Paintings; at a distance, they are all Nature, nearhand all Art, but both in extremest Beauty."

38

Pope, one of the early proponents of the new landscape style, created at Twickenham one of the first natural gardens. He gave practical expression to the new and still immature landscape movement and devised a garden that was to have far-reaching influence throughout the eighteenth century. In only five acres of land that had only a few trees when leased in 1719, Pope had, after eleven years of work and after spending up to £5000 annually, erected an orangery, a garden house, a grove, an obelisk in memory of his mother, a bowling green, a shell temple and a grotto. The grotto, the only remaining structure of Pope's garden, extended under the house like a basement and continued under the road behind the house to connect the garden and the river. The semicircular tunnel under the house, visible in the painting, was the grotto which was embellished with exotic gems and precious stones. Variety, irregularity, serpentine lines and elements of surprise, all prerequisites of the new landscape style, were incorporated here. Sir William Stanhope bought the house after Pope's death in 1744 and enlarged the villa with two bay wings to give it a more classical appearance (See Cat. 19). After 1807, it was purchased by Baroness Howe and later demolished.

This picture and its supposed companion painting of Secretary Johnston's House, which is apparently signed by J. Nickolls and dated 1726, have been a problem for scholars. Recent research and statements by Maynard Mack, Morris K. Brownell, and John Walker doubt the 1726 date; they suggest the present painting of Pope's Villa is based on a sketch by Augustine Heckell (?1690-1770) now in the Lewis-Walpole Library in Farmington, Connecticut, which was engraved by James Mason in 1749. This theory is based on the fact that the obelisk was not built until 1733 as a memorial to Pope's mother, who died that year; it was located behind the house in the actual garden rather than at the side as shown in the painting. Heckell's print is accurate. The Pantheon-like structure, also at the right, was not in Pope's garden but resembles the Shakespearean Temple built by David Garrick about 1755, nearby at Hampton. It has been suggested that if Nickolls was the artist, he did not actually see Twickenham and did not fully understand the layout of Pope's land. Whoever the artist, he probably copied the Heckell engraving, which was widely available, sometime after 1755.

18. Joseph Nickolls (active 1720–ca. 1755), ascribed to
ORLEANS HOUSE, TWICKENHAM, ca. 1755

Inscribed in ink, *J. Nickolls 1726*, lower left
Oil on canvas, 17¼ x 32 (43.8 x 81.4)
B1976.7.136
Coll: With Spink and Son from whom purchased 1960.
Lit: Christopher Hussey, "Twickenham II, Orleans House, The Octagon,"
    CL 96 (September 1944): 464-65; Walker 1969, p. 24

This house on the banks of the Thames at Twickenham was leased in 1702 to James Johnston, then Secretary of State for Scotland. In 1710 he employed the architect John James to build the house as seen in the painting in the Wren style with a mansard roof and a central doorway with stone detailing. The design for the facade appears in *Vitruvius Britannicus,* 1715.

The octagon pavilion at the left was designed and built by James Gibbs (1682-1754) in 1720 for the reception of Caroline of Ansbach (later Queen Caroline, wife of George II). Gibbs had recently returned from study with Carlo Fontana, the noted Baroque architect, in Italy and was soon afterwards to build the new church of St. Martin's-in-the-Fields, London, and later the Radcliffe Camera at Oxford. A connecting one-story gallery was built after 1727 as a passage between the main house and the octagonal garden pavilion. The small building to the far right is Ragman's Castle, lived in at various times by Mrs. Pritchard, the famous actress who worked with David Garrick, and Horace Walpole's niece, Maria, Lady Waldegrave.

After Johnston's death in 1737, the house was purchased by George Morton Pitt, once Governor of Fort St. George in the East Indies. A 1748 sketch by Augustine Heckell, engraved in 1749 by J. Mason, shows the house and grounds almost exactly as painted here. It has been suggested by John Walker (1969, p. 24) that Nickolls copied or drew his composition from the Heckell sketch, because the one-story connecting gallery was not built until after 1727 and this picture, dated 1726, shows it in place. The Nickolls signature, which appears genuine, and the impossibly early date were either drawn in by the artist (who might or might not be Nickolls) around 1755 when the painting was probably done, or they might be a later addition done by a dealer. See also *Pope's Villa* (Cat. 17) for a similar problem.

The name Orleans House dates from 1815-18, when King Louis-Philippe, then Duc d'Orleans (1773-1850) in exile from France, leased the house. It passed through many families and was finally demolished in 1926. The octagon was saved and remains on its original site.

19. Samuel Scott (1710-1772)
POPE'S VILLA, TWICKENHAM, ca. 1759

Oil on panel, 7½ x 14½ (19 x 36.2)
No. 1954
Coll: With Mount Street Enterprises, London, from whom purchased 1972
Exh: Kenneth Sharpe and Richard Kingsett, *Samuel Scott Bicentary (Catalogue of Paintings, Drawings, and Engravings)*, London, Guildhall Art Gallery, 1972, Cat. 46, repr. Pl. 46
Lit: Brownell 1978, Cat. 17; Harris 1979 (Cat. 362).

Pope's villa, as viewed from the northwest, is seen here with alterations made to the original design around 1759 by Sir William Stanhope (see Cat. 17). He bought the house in 1744 after the poet's death and added wings to both sides to give the building a more classical appearance. This painting is probably a sketch used by Scott for three larger versions, one of which is in the Lewis-Walpole Collection in Farmington, Connecticut.

Samuel Scott is best known as a marine painter but turned to topographical views, possibly through the success of Canaletto in England (1746-ca. 1756).

20. Richard Wilson, R.A. (1714-1782)
WILTON HOUSE, WILTSHIRE, FROM THE SOUTHEAST, ca. 1760

Oil on canvas, 39 x 56¾ (99 x 144)
No. 612
Coll: Benjamin Booth, sold Christie's May 30, 1809 (93); bt. in; Rev. R.S. Booth; Lady Ford; Rev. James Ford; Edmund Ford; Arthur Ford; with Sabin Galleries from whom purchased 1963
Exh: London, Tate Gallery, *Richard Wilson,* 1925 (59); V.M.F.A. 1963 (21) repr. Pl. 212; R.A. 1964-65 (52), repr. Pl. 70; Yale 1965 (222); Y.C.B.A. 1977 (27)
Lit: W.G. Constable, *Richard Wilson,* (London, 1953), pp. 188-89; *CL Annual* (1965), repr. p. 18

> "We went to Wilton House. This seat of the Pembroke family has
> been theirs two hundred years, but originally a monastery. Part of it
> was rebuilt in the reign of Henry VIII and part in that of Elizabeth.
> This charming tho' ancient mansion is situated in a garden of sixty
> acres, which a river runs thro'; a delightful lawn lays before the
> house, which has a view of the canal; a grand arcade at the upper end,
> where the fall of water is very fine. On the contrary, when you are at
> this building, the eye has still greater beauties to admire,, as the
> magnificent old structure, a Palladian Bridge, Gothic Seats, temples,
> and numberless pieces of the most pleasing objects in a fine
> prospect."

So wrote Mrs. Philip Lybbe Powys of Hardwick House on a visit to
Wilton House in 1759. This house was one of the most popular on
the tour circuit because of its romantic picturesque setting and its
great art collection. In 1758, 2,324 people came to see it and only
Stowe and Blenheim could boast more visitors. The first printed
guide for paintings, a modestly priced book intended for tourists,
was published here in 1731. It was followed later in the century by
several other guides to the house and grounds. Two of the major
attractions were the richly decorated "Single Cube" and "Double
Cube" rooms, the latter hung with several portraits by Van Dyck.

Wilton House is in Wiltshire located near the town of Wilton
at the junction of the rivers Nadder and Wiley. An abbey was first
built here in 773, and the site remained in religious hands until the
dissolution of the monasteries under Henry VIII. The land was then
granted by the King to Sir William Herbert, who was made Earl of
Pembroke in 1560 by Edward VI. The first Earl built a Tudor house
which was rebuilt by the 4th Earl of Pembroke in 1636. It was
designed by Isaac de Caus with improvements apparently supervised by Inigo Jones. The house has a symmetrical facade of nine
bays with two projecting end bays; the only embellishment besides
the mouldings are the figures carved in relief above the central
window. This classical facade was an inspiration to eighteenth-
century architects; yet, through Colen Campbell's attribution exclu-
sively to Inigo Jones in *Vitruvius Britannicus,* de Caus's part was
forgotten. Wilton House provided the inspiration for at least three
Georgian houses: Houghton, Hagley, and Croome (Hill and Cornforth 1966, pp. 75–86).

In the seventeenth century, the house had a large formal
garden. By the mid-eighteenth century, the grounds had been

"improved" to reflect changing taste in landscape. The 9th Earl altered the house in the 1730s and, with the help of architect Roger Morris, built the Palladian Bridge. Vertue mentions it after a visit in 1740, saying, "The bridge is very elegant and fine fronting the house. This is the design of the present Earl of Pembroke and built under his direction, so much skill in the art of architecture by a nobleman does great Honour to the Art" (Vertue, 5, p. 130). The bridge was an inspiration for other such structures and was copied frequently in other gardens. The bridge form also came to be used as a garden folly with the fanciful intention of conveying the viewer to Arcadia, or an ancient abbey, or Arthur's Court.

This painting is an unfinished sketch of Wilton House from across the River Nadder. There is a finished and signed version of approximately the same size dated 1760 (Earl of Pembroke Collection) as well as two other versions. In these paintings, Wilson has treated the house as an excuse for a Claudian landscape bathed in an evening glow, rather than as an accurate representation of the house. Although Wilson painted a few house portraits early in his career, his classical landscape style was not suitable for commissioned works whose major interest was purely topographical.

21. George Barret, Senior, R.A. (1732-1784)
A VIEW OF POWERSCOURT, COUNTY WICKLOW, IRELAND, ca. 1760-62

Oil on canvas, 28⅞ x 38¼ (73.4 x 97.2)
No. 802
Coll: Col. M.H. Grant; with M. Bernard, 1963; with Gooden & Fox from
      whom purchased 1963, as by Thomas Roberts
Exh: London, Arts Council, *Early English Landscapes*, 1952-53 (47) as by
      Thomas Roberts; Belfast, Ulster Museum, and Dublin, Municipal
      Gallery of Modern Art, *Irish Houses and Landscapes,* 1963 (43) as by
      Thomas Roberts, repr. Pl. 4; Y.C.B.A. 1977 (26)
Lit: M. H. Grant, *Old English Landscape Painters* (London, 1925), p. 91, repr.
      p. 57 as by Thomas Roberts; Guinness and Ryan 1971, repr. p. 324;
      Harris 1979 (Cat. 309).

"You look full upon the house, which appears to be in the most beautiful situation in the world on the side of a mountain halfway between its bare top and an irregious vale at its foot. In front and spreading among wood on either side is a lawn whose surface is beautifully varied in gentle declivities, hanging to a winding river."

Arthur Young wrote this description of Powerscourt in *A Tour of Ireland* (Dublin, 1780). The house is located in Enniskerry, County Wicklow in the Dargle Valley beneath Sugarloaf Mountain. In the fourteenth century the land belonged to the Bishopric of Glendalough. Eustace de la Powere probably built a castle here and thus gave the site its name. The castle passed from family to family, and was destroyed and rebuilt many times before it was granted by James I in 1609 to Sir Richard Wingfield, who had successfully quelled a rebellion in Londonderry the previous year. In 1618, the King bestowed the title of Viscount Powerscourt on Richard Wingfield. A distant cousin, also named Richard Wingfield and the 3rd Viscount Powerscourt, built the house seen here in 1730-43.

Typical of the Irish baroque style, the architect, Richard Cassels, expanded the facade to create the maximum effect. The central block has a wide pediment supported on seven Tuscan pilasters. On either side, a corridor runs to smaller wings, which housed the stables to the left and the kitchen to the right. Beyond this are curved curtain walls which end in obelisks surmounted by the Wingfield eagle. Powerscourt House is a fine example of Irish baroque architecture with its classical and exuberant prolonged facade (Guinness and Ryan, *Irish Houses,* pp. 324-25).

The landscape sweeps right up to the house. By the mid-eighteenth century, the English landscape style had spread into Ireland, making terraces, fountains and flower beds obsolete. Powerscourt, with its waterfall and magnificent setting, was one of the most popular places on the country house tour circuit. The house, still standing and privately owned, was gutted by fire in 1977.

The painting has been attributed to the Irish artist, Thomas Roberts, and to George Barret, Jr., but seems more certainly by the elder George Barret. He was born in Dublin and studied art there, where he was noticed by Edmund Burke, who encouraged him to paint landscapes. Barret often sketched at Powerscourt and painted three other views of the house and surrounding countryside in the early 1760s. He was not well received in Ireland, but after moving to London in 1762, became an established landscapist. He was also one of the founders of the Royal Academy.

22. Francis Harding (active 1740–ca. 1766), attributed to
A VIEW OF WARWICK CASTLE, ca. 1764

Oil on canvas, 24¾ x 39¼ (62.9 x 99.5)
B1976.7.34
Coll: In a private collection, Ireland; with Leggatt Brothers from whom
purchased in 1972
Lit: David Jacques, "Capability Brown at Warwick Castle," *CL* 165
(February 22, 1979): 475, repr.

David Jacques has pointed out that this view of Warwick
represents Lancelot "Capability" Brown's newly completed landscaping around the castle carried out for Francis Greville, Lord
Brooke (1719-73). The owner, like many of his contemporaries,
desired his surroundings to "avoid Formality, Regularity and Stiff-
ness" (cited by Jacques, p. 476). Thus, from 1749 until 1760, Brown
executed a plan that softened "the relationship of castle, gardens and
park" (p. 475), and masked the town from view. He removed the old
formal gardens, planted trees in pairs or clumps (evident on the
island, Castle Meadow, in the foreground) and also planted shrubs
on the artificial mound with its spiral path by the west wall of the
castle (left). A similar composition of Warwick painted by Canaletto
in 1749 (Lord Astor of Hever Collection) shows the sparsely planted
setting before its transformation by Brown, as well as a wooden
bridge which was removed by the time of this painting.

On a cliff above the River Avon, Warwick was the site of a
fortified manor built in 1068 by William the Conqueror. The mound
against the west wall, dating from the same period, is named after
Ethelfleda, the daughter of King Alfred, who is said to have built the
first stronghold on the site. A stone structure was erected in the
twelfth or thirteenth century by unknown medieval architects, and
by the late fifteenth century, the castle with its stone towers had
assumed its present shape. It was granted by James I to the Greville
family in 1604 and remained in their possession until recently. The
owners continued to renovate and add to Warwick through the
nineteenth century. For instance, the sashed windows shown in this
view, were to be reconstructed in the Gothic style.

Francis Harding (active 1740-ca. 1766), to whom this scene is
attributed, began his career as a carriage painter. According to
George Vertue, he "happily" followed the manner of Pannini and
Canaletto, whose views he imitated "with good success" (Vertue 3,

p. 127). With the exception of the landscaping, the views of Warwick by Canaletto and this artist are nearly identical in vantage point and composition. Harding's original work is little known: one example is his *Interior of the Church of St. John the Evangelist,*ca. 1744 (Hilda Finberg, "Francis Harding: a Forgotten Painter of Architecture," *CL* 47 [May 1, 1920], repr. p. 597).

23. British School, XVIII Century
KIDBROOKE PARK, KENT, ca. 1770

Oil on canvas, 30 x 45¼ (73 x 115)
No. 925
Coll: D.W. Freshfield; Captain R. Olaf Hambro; with Thos. Agnew &
    Sons from whom purchased 1964
Lit: Harris 1979 (Cat. 279), as by George Lambert, ca. 1740s.

Kidbrooke House, situated about forty miles from London at the edge of the Ashdown Forest, was built in 1733-34 by William Nevill, the 16th Earl of Abergavenny. The building was designed by an unknown follower of William Kent and Lord Burlington and shows characteristics of their style. The most notable feature of the design is the massive group of chimney stacks rising from the central block. This painting shows the house situated in the hollow of a narrow valley surrounded by trees with an orderly forecourt garden area. The house and grounds were dramatically altered after 1805 when Charles Abbot, later Lord Colchester, bought the property. The well known Speaker of the House of Commons commissioned Humphrey Repton to improve the landscape; the forecourt was replaced by a winding approach and the trees were moved or taken out to create new vistas and views ("Kidbrooke Park, Forest Row, Sussex," *CL* 79 [April 18, 1936]: 404-409).

This painting was formerly attributed to George Lambert, but many characteristics, particularly the treatment of the foliage, have made that attribution doubtful. It is probably the work of a provincial artist and is reminiscent of earlier bird's-eye views. The painting is dated ca. 1770 by the costume of the figures.

24. British School, XVIII Century, possibly Theodore De Bruyn
(1730-1804)
THE HERMITAGE, ca. 1770-76

Oil on canvas, 32½ x 51⅜ (82.5 x 131)
No. 544
Coll: With Sabin Galleries from whom purchased 1960
Exh: V.M.F.A. 1963 (14), repr. Pl. 122; R.A. 1964-65 (45), repr. Pl. 46; Yale
    1965 (202); Y.C.B.A. 1977 (143), repr.
Lit: Harris 1979 (Cat. 365) as attributed to Theodore de Bruyn

Hermitage House was located three miles southwest towards
Fulham from the center of London at the corner of Lillie and North
End Roads, in the village of North End, as it was known at the time.
It was bought and rebuilt by the actor and dramatist Samuel Foote
(1720-1777) in 1767 to be used as his country retreat. Between 1769
and 1776, Foote rented a narrow strip of land behind the house
known as Marshcroft, in which he developed a small vegetable
garden as well as pleasure walks through orchards (C.J. Fèret,
Fulham, Old and New, 3 vols. [London, 1900], 2: 269, 271). It was at
the Hermitage, in its rural situation with a grassy expanse of land
between the house and the city, that Foote entertained friends. In the
distance can be seen St. Paul's, Westminster Abbey, and the Church
of St. John, Smith Square.

According to John Harris, the artist of this painting may be
Theodore de Bruyn, who came to England about 1760. De Bruyn·
was a leading painter of sculptural ornaments, although he also
executed views of country houses which were exhibited at the Royal
Academy between 1773-1803.

25. Dominic Serres, R.A. (1722-1793)
SAINT VINCENT, KENT, THE SEAT OF CAPT. WILLIAM
LOCKER, ca. 1779-80

Signed, *D. Serres 17[ ]*, lower left
Oil on canvas, 12½ x 18 (31.7 x 45.7)
No. 1098
Coll: Commissioned by Capt. William Locker; possibly given by him to a
    member of the Stratford family; Wingfield Stratford, Addington,
    Kent; his sale (date unknown); bt. H. G. Hewlett; given by him to a
    grandson of Capt. Locker; anonymous sale, Christie's, April 17,
    1964 (84); bt. P. & D. Colnaghi, from whom purchased in 1964
Lit: Harris 1979 (Cat. 305).

An old label on the reverse of the painting, written by a
member of the Locker family, traces the picture's past ownership
and identifies the house as "St. Vincents, my grandfather's place in
Kent." Presumably the family of Capt. William Locker (1731-1800)
stands before the house, including his wife Lucy, two daughters, and
three sons. His youngest son, Edward Hawke Locker, was born in
1777, and Mrs. Locker died in 1780, thus dating the picture shortly
before that time. Locker retired from active service in the Navy in
1779 due to ill-health and inherited the house from his father-in-law
in the same year. The brick, hipped-roof house with its pedimented
doorway was situated in Addington, two miles east of Wrotham and
seven miles northwest of Maidstone, Kent, overlooking Addington Brook (W. H. Ireland, *A New and Complete History of the County
of Kent,* 4 vols., [London, 1829-30], 3:617). According to the label,
Locker may have sold St. Vincent when he was appointed lieutenant
governor of Greenwich Hospital in 1793. He is noted as the teacher
and friend of the young Horatio Nelson, who wrote to him in 1799:
"our friendship will never end but with my life" (DNB).

Dominic Serres, who painted mostly marine subjects, was a
friend of Locker's (according to the label on the painting), and had
painted his portrait in 1769 (Y.C.B.A., Paul Mellon Collection).
John Thomas Serres (1759-1825) the artist's son, may have accom-
panied his father when the older artist painted this picture, for in
1780 the youth exhibited at the Royal Academy a watercolor of the
Abbey in nearby Malling, Kent.

26. William Ashford, R.H.A. (1746-1824)
GEORGIAN HOUSE IN A LANDSCAPE, ca. 1775-80

Oil on canvas, 30 x 42 (76 x 106.5)
No. 2196
Coll: Sold Bonham's, April 1, 1965 (68); with Thos. Agnew & Sons from
    whom purchased 1965
Lit: Anne O. Crookshank, "Irish Landscapes with an English Air, William
    Ashford," *CL* 157 (May 22, 1975): 1353, repr. Pl. 5; Harris 1979 (Cat.
    342).

The identity of this house is not known. Its distinguishing
feature is the pediment, which is enclosed in the second story beneath
the roof line. The house does not dominate the carefully ordered
landscape but sits among a cluster of trees on a small hill. The trees
have been artfully cut away to allow the owner a view of the green

lawn, which gradually becomes melded into the gently rolling landscape. This painting, which has also been called *Landscape with
Haymakers,* is typical of Ashford's quiet style, which tended to
concentrate on topography.

27. William Ashford, R.H.A. (1746-1824)
    MOUNT KENNEDY, COUNTY WICKLOW, IRELAND, 1785

Signed, *WAshford/1785,* lower right
Oil on canvas, 16^9/16 x 24^1/16 (42.1 x 61.1)
B1976.7.92
Coll: With Frank T. Sabin from whom purchased 1967
Lit: Harris 1979 (Cat. 339).
Engravings: Thomas Milton, 1787

The house, located about seventeen miles southeast of Dublin,
was built by a General Cunninghame about 1784, after his purchase
of the 10,000 acres from Elizabeth Barker. She had inherited the land
from the last male heir of the Kennedy family; the estate retained the
Kennedy name. The house itself has been referred to as Hull House,
after a Mr. Hull who lived there later.

In 1772 General Cunninghame first commissioned James
Wyatt (1746-1813) to draw up plans for his new house. The English
architect had achieved notoriety as the designer of the Pantheon in
London, which first opened in 1770. Construction of Mount
Kennedy, however, was delayed for more than ten years, while
Cunninghame extensively landscaped its grounds (Guinness and
Ryan 1971, p. 315). In 1787, Thomas Milton published an engraving
of Mount Kennedy after this painting in his *Collection of Select Views
from Different Seats in Ireland,* and dated the house 1784. He stated that
it was executed by a Mr. Cooley after Wyatt's design. Since Cooley,
however, died in 1784, the house must have been started before that
date. His apprentice architect, Francis Johnston, then supervised the
construction of the house.

Thomas Milton described the famous site of Mount Kennedy
in his book:

"At distances from the Demesne, are Parts which present the most
striking Scenes of Natural Beauties and Ruggedness; on those, the
vigorous and elegant Taste of the Proprietor has been exerted, to
render them worthy of the Notice of Travellers; . . . there are,
perhaps, few places in Ireland superior in Beauty to Mount Kennedy.

The whole estate has been indefatigably improved; that Part on which the house stands has been finished, and is preserved with extraordinary Taste and Care."

The "indefatigably improved" landscape dominates the painting. The lawn extends up to the house, and vistas have been cut through the trees to allow the most beautiful view both toward the house and out into the magnificent countryside. The "genius of the place" has been consciously consulted and the house sited according to the flow of the land and the most romantic and spectacular view possible.

William Ashford was born in Birmingham in 1746, and went to Ireland in 1764 to work in Dublin for the Ordnance Office. It is not known where or if he received painting instruction, but by 1767, he had become a full-time artist. Ashford became the most popular landscape painter in Ireland in the late eighteenth century and was renowned for his pictures of country houses. He was elected the first President of the Royal Hibernian Academy in 1823 and died in 1824.

28. Thomas Gooch (active 1778-1802)
HON. MARCIA AND HON. GEORGE PITT, RIDING IN THE PARK OF STRATFIELD SAYE HOUSE, HAMPSHIRE, 1782

Signed, *Thos. Gooch/ 1782*, lower right
Oil on canvas, 27 x 25 (68.6 x 63.5)
No. 1640
Coll: By descent to James Lane-Fox, Bramham Park, Wetherby, Yorkshire; by descent to Sir Edward Vavasour, Hazelwood, Yorkshire; with Gooden & Fox from whom purchased in 1963
Exh: Probably Royal Academy, 1783 (116) as *Portraits of a Young Nobleman and his Sister on horseback;* R.A. 1964-65 (242), repr. Pl. 29; Yale 1965 (97).
Lit: Stella A. Walker, *Sporting Art, England 1700-1900* (New York, 1972, p. 89, repr. Pl. 50.; Egerton (Cat. 141).

The artist represents Stratfield Saye, the country seat of the Pitt family, by fitting a view of it into the space between the horse's legs—an odd but effective method of combining house and equestrian portraits on a canvas of small dimensions.

The riders, George Pitt (1751-1828), and his sister Marcia, were the children of George Pitt (1721-1803), 1st Baron Rivers who, in 1745, had inherited immense land holdings as well as Stratfield Saye. During the following decades, Lord Rivers greatly modified and enlarged the Caroline brick house which had been built around 1640 by his ancestor, Sir William Pitt. On the east, or garden side (shown in the painting), Pitt added canted bay windows on the outer bays and filled in the central section, with its four-columned porch and pediment, between the old Dutch-gabled wings. The cupola, later removed, was restored in 1964 based on its original appearance in eighteenth-century views.

In 1817, after the Battle of Waterloo, a grateful nation purchased the house from George Pitt and presented it to the Duke of Wellington, who made further alterations to the house, and whose descendants are still in residence there. In 1830, J. Hewetson (*Architectural Views of Noble Mansions in Hampshire* [London]) described the east front of Stratfield Saye as opening out to:

> "a beautiful lawn, sloping to a noble piece of water, interspersed with islands covered with trees. Noble avenues stretch for miles over the domaine which abounds with the finest timber, while the adjacent country consists of open downs, affording pasture for large flocks of sheep."

Gooch painted a nearly identical version of this portrait, dated 1782 (size unknown), which was in the Pitt-Rivers Collection around 1895 (sold at Christie's, January 12, 1901). In 1782 Gooch exhibited a painting of horses and dogs owned by Lord Rivers, as well as a portrait of the latter on a "managed horse." A little-known artist, Gooch exhibited nearly every year between 1781-1802 with the Royal Academy.

29. William Marlow (1740-1813), attributed to
GEORGIAN HOUSE ON A COMMON, ca. 1785-94

Oil on canvas, 26¼ x 33¼ (66.5 x 84.5)
No. 2205
Coll: With Frank T. Sabin from whom purchased 1965
Lit: Harris 1979 (Cat. 319) as by an unknown artist.

Formerly identified incorrectly as Little Marble Hill, Twickenham, this unknown house is typical of a number of detached residences on the outskirts of London from the middle of the eighteenth century. Its use of quoins and rusticated columns may have been based on designs published in contemporary pattern books available to a middle-class market.

Villages developed along the River Thames to accommodate increasing numbers of people who wanted to be near the city and not within it. Such places are described in the "Foreigner's Guide to London" published in 1740.

> "The River on both sides down to London is full of villages as Isleworth, Twickenham, Petersham, Richmond, Chiswick, Mortlake, Barn Elms, Fulham, Putney, Hammersmith, Battersea, and Chelsea, and many more and all these villages are full of beautiful buildings being country houses of noblemen, gentlemen and indeed tradesmen of the City of London."

Smaller suburban houses were often built in the prevailing style of their larger country house counterparts.

30. George Cuitt, Senior (1743–1818)
VIEW OF EASBY HALL, EASBY ABBEY, AND THE PARISH CHURCH WITH RICHMOND, YORKSHIRE, IN THE BACKGROUND, ca. 1790–1810

Oil on canvas, 40⅛ x 69 (101.9 x 175.2)
B1976.7.92
Coll: John Close (dates unknown), Easby Hall; by descent to his daughter Anna who married, in 1777, William Tufnell (1749–1812), of Langleys, Chelmsford, Essex; by descent in the Tufnell family; with Edward Speelman from whom purchased 1971.
Lit: Christopher Hussey, "Yorkshire Scenes 150 Years Ago, Paintings of Country Life at Langleys," *CL* 92 (September 18, 1942):553 repr. as by Joseph Farington; Harris 1979 (Cat. 329).

The painting descended in the family of John Close, the owner of Easby Hall, which is represented on the hillside at the far right, overlooking the ruins of Easby Abbey, the River Swale, and Richmond, one mile away to the northwest. Despite its distance from the viewer, the scene is shown in meticulous detail, including the obelisk in the market place at Richmond. Pevsner describes Easby Hall as a "charming, ingenuous early nineteenth-century house," with seven bays, a widely spaced three bay center, and a one bay pediment. It is probable, however, that the house was built in the last decade of the eighteenth century. Since the south front of the house matches Pevsner's description only in the wide spacing of the windows, it is possible that Cuitt executed his painting before subsequent additions were erected on either side of the south front.

The painting, formerly attributed to Joseph Farington, is now reattributed to the elder Cuitt, who spent the last forty years of his life painting landscapes and country house views around his native Richmond. A slightly smaller version of this painting by Cuitt, without the foreground figures, was with Spink & Son, London, in 1976. He also painted a nearly identical view of the ruined abbey (named for St. Agatha and founded in 1152) with Richmond in the background which is presently attributed to his son, George Cuitt the Younger (National Gallery of Art, Washington).

31. John Bird of Liverpool (1768-1829)
STREET SCENE IN CHORLEY, LANCASHIRE, WITH A VIEW OF CHORLEY HALL, ca. 1790-1817

Oil on canvas, 11½ x 15½ (29.24 x 39.5)
No. 2193
Coll: With Gooden & Fox from whom purchased 1965

Chorley Hall, seen in the middle background of this painting, was located approximately half a mile outside the industrial town of Chorley, Lancashire. The house, built about 1717, descended through the Chorley family until it was sold to Abraham Crompton in 1746, who rebuilt it. The front of the house probably faces the viewer because, as shown in the Ordnance Survey map of 1846, the entrance and drive were situated in the clearing. Lending support to its identity as Chorley Hall is a contemporary description of it as a "fine stone gabled edifice" (letter from J.D. Farquhar, Librarian, Lancashire County Council to John Harris, September 19, 1978).

The scene represented here is of Church Brow, seen from Market Street. The building behind the cart, on Hollinshead Street, is the Swan Inn which remains standing today. Chorley Hall was torn down in 1817 and none of the other buildings survives.

John Bird, a Liverpool native, was a self-taught artist. As a landscapist he provided drawings for Angus's *Views of the Seats* (London, 1787). In addition he practised as an architect and surveyor: his only recorded work is St. Nicholas Church in Liverpool, ca. 1810.

32. British School XVIII or XIX Century
LEE PRIORY, KENT, ca. 1800

Oil on canvas, 25 x 38¾ (63.5 x 98.4)
B1975.1.8
Coll: With W. J. Gaskin, London, from whom purchased 1970
Lit: Harris 1979 (Cat. 382) as attributed to Hendrik de Cort.

> "You will see a child of Strawbery prettier than the parent and so executed and so finished! There is a delicious closet, too, so flattering to me; and a prior's library so antique, and that does so much honour to Mr. Wyatt's taste."

So wrote Horace Walpole to the Berry sisters in 1794 of Lee Priory, a house designed for his friend Thomas Barrett by James Wyatt (1746-1813). Barrett, whose father had amassed a notable art collection, was educated at Trinity College, Cambridge, and went on the Grand Tour through Europe and Italy. He returned to England in 1773, had the old seventeenth-century house demolished, and commissioned James Wyatt to build a Gothic house with a Grecian dining room. Work was begun in 1783 and was not completed until just after Barrett's death in 1803 (Hugh Honour, "A House of the Gothic Revival," *CL* 111 [May 30, 1952], pp. 1665-66).

The first Gothic Revival house to show technical understanding of the medieval style and its workings, Lee Priory was a step beyond Strawberry Hill, which was designed and created almost entirely by an amateur. This view shows the south range, terminated at one end by a square tower and, at the other, by an octagonal structure containing the library. The octagon became a popular form in the early nineteenth century because of its romantic, Gothic and generally exotic associations. This example has mullioned windows and a balustraded spire. The name Lee Priory was probably suggested by Thomas Barrett, who spoke of a sense of monastic seclusion there. The house was later altered by Sir Gilbert Scott, who elaborated upon its Gothic style. It was demolished in 1955 but a portion of the interior was re-erected in the Victoria and Albert Museum in London. The park surrounding the house was highly praised for being simple, serene and austere.

33. Samuel De Wilde (ca. 1751-1832), attributed to
A GENTLEMAN IN THE GROUNDS OF HIS HOUSE, ca.
1800-10

Oil on canvas, 23¾ x 19¾ (60.5 x 50)
No. 999
Coll: General Bulwer, Heydon Hall, Norfolk; sold Christie's, November
22, 1963 (117) as by Mortimer; bt. P. & D. Colnaghi from whom
purchased in 1963
Exh: R. A. 1964-65 (207); Yale 1965 (77)

Neither the man in the portrait nor his setting has been
identified. In the background are a three-story Georgian house and
an unusual garden pavilion with a bowed central projection surmounted by a dome. Possibly the latter structure was a new addition
to the park at the time of the painting.

De Wilde, born in London of Dutch parents, made his repu-
tation by painting small full-length portraits of actors and actresses
in theatrical costumes, enacting their roles in contemporary plays.
He exhibited many of these with the Royal Academy from 1792 until
1821 (see Ian Mayes, *The De Wildes,* Northampton Central Art
Gallery, 1971). Occasionally, however, he also painted non-theatrical
individual and group portraits.

34. British School, XIX Century
COUNTRY HOUSE IN A RIVER LANDSCAPE, ca. 1800-12

Oil on canvas, 34½ x 45½ (87.5 x 115.5)
No. 241
Coll: R.D. Trafford, Esq.; with Leggatt Brothers from whom purchased in
1960 as by Paul Sandby

This crenellated house was formerly thought to be Oatlands
near Esher, Surrey, a house built in the Tudor style in the early
seventeenth century. Oatlands was later remodelled, but there is no
evidence that it resembled the house in this painting. This house
probably dates from the early nineteenth century, with the facade
combining elements of a Tudor castle and an Italianate villa. Castellated houses like Downton Castle, near Ludlow, built by Richard
Payne Knight in 1774-78, and the Italian villa style seen in Cronkhill
in Salop, designed by John Nash in 1802, may have provided the
inspiration.

The garden reflects the influence of Humphrey Repton, whose ideas lead to the reestablishment of flower beds near the house on a terrace, and the planting of trees in clumps.

35. Thomas Daniell, R.A. (1749-1840)
A VIEW OF THE TEMPLE, FOUNTAIN, AND CAVE AT SEZINCOTE PARK, GLOUCESTERSHIRE, 1819

Signed, *T. Daniell-1819,* on rock, lower left
Oil on canvas, 39¾ x 50 (101 x 127)
No. 2548
Coll: Major J.M.E. Askew; sold Christie's June 17, 1966 (45); bt. P. & D.
    Colnaghi from whom purchased 1966
Exh: Royal Academy, 1819 (357); Y.C.B.A. 1977 (144)
Lit: J.P. Neale, *Views of the Seats of Noblemen . . . ,* 6 vols. (London, 1818-23),
    2: n.p.; Thomas Sutton, *The Daniells* (London, 1954), p. 95.

Sezincote, the Gloucestershire house of Charles Cockerell, was one of the first examples of the Indian style in England. Cockerell had returned from his post with the East India Company in 1804 and wanted to recreate his Indian experience in England. He commissioned his architect brother, Samuel Pepys Cockerell (ca. 1754-1827), to build the house with the help of Thomas and William Daniell's drawings of Indian buildings. (For a view of the house, see Anne Rushout's sketchbook, Cat. 89).

The garden seen here was probably a collaboration between the artist, Thomas Daniell, and the garden architect, Humphrey Repton. The picturesque garden shows Indian influences, such as the temple dedicated to the Sun God Souriya which stands above the Voltinus Pool. A fountain in the midst of the basin spouts water which flows over in cascades toward the viewer. Rockwork caves, common in India, have been cut into the hill behind the temple. This garden was perhaps the inspiration for the Prince Regent in his decision to "Indianize" the Royal Pavilion at Brighton. Having seen Sezincote (probably in 1807), he commissioned Humphrey Repton to design a building, but the final structure was executed by John Nash and begun in 1815. The resulting pavilion at Brighton is a fanciful and imaginative interpretation of Indian architecture.

Thomas Daniell and his nephew William (1769-1837) were among the first British artists to travel to India. They arrived in Calcutta in 1786 and travelled all over India and to China in 1793. They made a great number of drawings, some pencil sketches, sepia or blue grey wash drawings and pure watercolors. These drawings, some of which belonged to Charles Cockerell, were important for the dissemination of the Indian style. This painting is one of six views of Sezincote that Daniell exhibited at the Royal Academy in 1818 and 1819.

36. John Constable, R.A. (1776-1837)
MALVERN HALL, WARWICKSHIRE, ca. 1821

Oil on canvas, 21½ x 30¾ (54 x 78)
B1977.14.43
Coll: Isabel Constable; sold Christie's, June 17, 1892 (265); bt. Gooden, London; Cheramy Sale, Paris, 1908; Gerstenberg, Berlin; Dr. Fritz Nathan, Zurich; Dr. Robert Buhler, Winterthur, Switzerland; with E.V. Thaw and Co., New York from whom purchased 1977
Lit: London, Tate Gallery, *John Constable,* 1976, referred to in Cats. 88 and 202; *Solihull News,* No. 2254, Saturday July 8, 1978, repr. p. 18.

This Warwickshire house was the seat of Henry Greswolde Lewis (1754-1829), who commissioned several works from Constable over twenty years. The artist was probably introduced to Lewis by Magdalene, Dowager Countess of Dysart, Lewis's sister. Constable visited Malvern Hall twice: in 1809 to paint Mary Freer, the Lewis's thirteen year old ward (Y.C.B.A., Paul Mellon Collection) and to sketch the house. In 1820 he returned to paint several versions of the house.

Begun by Humphrey Greswold around 1690, Malvern Hall was radically altered for Henry Lewis after 1783 by the young architect, John Soane, who was then working in the neoclassical style. Originally the house was a seven bay building with a pedimented central feature. Soane added a shallow curved porch with Ionic columns which is visible in the painting. Henry Lewis was annoyed with these changes. He replaced much of Soane's work and proceeded with further alterations *(Malvern Hall, Warwickshire, From Stately Home to School* [privately published, ca. 1970], pp. 26-29). He invited Constable back to see and paint the house, writing to the artist in 1819 that "Malverne is going on, & is much improved inside & out, & would make a much better figure in Landscape than when you painted it last" *(John Constable's Correspondence,* ed. R.B. Beckett, 6 vols. [Ipswich, 1962-68], 4:64).

As a result of his 1820-21 visit, Constable seems to have produced three views of the front of the house, all of which are similar. In addition to the present example, a version is in the Sterling and Francine Clark Art Institute, Williamstown, Massachusetts, and another is in the Musée de Tesse, Le Mans, France. It has been suggested recently by Michael Tollemache (letters dated May 30, 1977 and June 23, 1977), who has had access to family papers, that this picture as the most painterly and freely drawn of the three, was done for the artist himself. He further suggests that the Williamstown painting, which remained in the family until the early twentieth century, was commissioned as a topographical record of the house and its setting, and is not a copy as suggested in the Tate Gallery Constable exhibition, 1976 (Cat. 22). The publication of the Dysart papers may help to identify the different versions. Constable was not happy with strictly topographical commissions and may have acquiesced in this instance in deference to Lady Dysart, an early patron.

37. Patrick Nasmyth (1787-1831)
PENSHURST PLACE, KENT, ca. 1824-30

Signed, *Pat. Nasmyth,* lower left
Oil on panel, 18 x 24 (45.5 x 61)
No. 120
Coll: With P. & D. Colnaghi from whom purchased 1962.

Among the trees in the background lies Penshurst Place, a predominantly Tudor and Elizabethan structure lying on the north bank of the upper Medway. This is the southern view of the house shown with its grey walls made of native stone and brick, ornamental chimneys, square embattled towers and tiled roofs. To the left lies the village of Penshurst dominated by the church tower. As in many paintings of country houses at this time, the artist included a more comprehensive view than can be seen from one vantage point.

Penshurst was a manor house, acquired in 1338 by the London merchant Sir John de Pultney during the time of Edward III. He created the hall and state dining room which still remain today. Later the house was enlarged by Sir John Devereux and by the 1st Duke of Buckingham. In 1547 the house became the possession of Edward VI. Five years later he granted Penshurst to Sir William Sidney, his "trustye, and wellbeloved servant," as is inscribed on a stone tablet over the porch of the gatehouse. The house has remained in the possession of the Sidneys to the present day. In spite of additions and renovations of the house over a period of five centuries, much of the original architecture remains. By the early 1800s Penshurst had fallen into neglect, and restoration work was started. John Shelley began repairs on the building in 1818 which continued through succeeding generations. In the mid-nineteenth century, the 2nd Lord De L'Isle and Dudley carefully renovated the formal gardens at the south of the house along the lines of the old garden, so that a view of it today bears a close resemblance to the view in Kip's engraving of 1707.

Patrick Nasmyth, eldest son of the artist, Alexander, was a landscape painter of Scottish and later English views. The date of this painting is based on Nasmyth's style, as well as on the fact that he exhibited two Kentish landscapes at the British Institution in 1824 and 1830.

38. James Ward, R.A. (1769-1859)
CATTLE AT A POOL AT SUNRISE, 1827

Signed, *J.W.R.A. 1827,* lower left
Oil on paper laid on board, 12¼ x 17¾ (31 x 45.5)
No. 2093
Coll: With Gooden & Fox from whom purchased 1965

The building depicted here is thought by Edward Nygren to be Tabley House, Cheshire, which Turner also sketched. The Palladian style house was built for Sir Peter Leicester in 1762-1769. It was designed by the Yorkshire architect, John Carr of York (1723-1807), who rivalled John Paine as a builder of country houses in the Midlands and the North of England. A grand temple front portico in the Greek style dominated the design.

This small painting, which shows the house from the side, is probably a sketch done by Ward in preparation for a larger canvas. The artist painted several pictures for Sir John Fleming Leicester, later 1st Lord Tabley (1762-1827), including a drawing in this exhibition (Cat. 84), but a topographical representation of the house was not his major interest. Ward was known chiefly as a painter of animals and romantic landscapes sometimes in the manner of Rubens. He became a member of the Royal Academy in 1811.

39. George Chinnery, R.H.A. (1774-1852)
AN ENGLISH FAMILY IN MACAO, ca. 1835-40

Oil on canvas, 28⅜ x 23⅛ (72 x 58.5)
No. 2206
Coll: Hahn and Son, London; sold to Frank T. Sabin from whom purchased
1965

The identity of the family (and the country house represented on the wall behind them) is unknown. They are probably Scottish, however, to judge by the boy's tartan, and they undoubtedly lived in the Portuguese colony of Macao where Chinnery worked from 1825 until his death in 1852. The family's expatriate life far from England is underscored by the ship under sail in the left distance, and by the sheet music under the window which has inscribed in its title the word "EXILE." They had probably brought the painting of the house with

them to Macao as a reminder of home. It appears to be an example of neo-classical domestic architecture in the style of Samuel Wyatt (1737-

1807), who specialized in medium-sized country houses with prominently bowed projections.

Chinnery executed a nearly identical oil sketch of this portrait but with the mother replaced by a young Chinese nurse, a dog under the sofa and a landscape view out of the window, left, instead of a seascape (Christie's, March 17, 1978, lot 60; repr. in Praz 1971, Pl. 311). An identical house is shown in the background of that painting.

40. James Holland (1800-1870)
THE LADY BETTY GERMAIN BEDROOM AT KNOLE, KENT, 184[?5]

Signed, *J. Holland 184[?5]*, lower right
Oil on canvas, 27 x 37⅝ (68.5 x 95.5)
B1976.7.43
Coll: With J. & S. Maas from whom purchased 1971

One of the largest country seats in England, Knole was owned by the Sackville family until 1947. Originally a small manor house, it was first enlarged by Thomas Bourchier, Archbishop of

Canterbury, who bought the house in 1456, and then altered by Thomas Sackville, who was granted the house in 1566 by Elizabeth I. Knole has remained virtually and remarkably unchanged for the last three centuries. Built of grey Kentish ragstone, it has seven main courtyards which divide and link the various parts of the house, and a complicated interior which, according to legend, consists of fifty-two staircases and 365 rooms. It was, nevertheless, described by Horace Walpole as a house of "beautiful decent simplicity which charms one" (V. Sackville-West, *Knole and the Sackvilles* [London, 1958], p. 18).

Lady Betty Germain (1680-1769), second wife of Sir John Germain, was a friend and companion of Lionel, 1st Duke of Dorset (1686-1765) and his wife Elizabeth, and she lived at Knole during their lifetime. The two rooms at Knole were thus given her name. Known for her accomplished needlework, she worked on curtains, hangings, and covers of chairs not only for her own room, but also for other rooms in the house.

This interior is thought to be one of the two rooms once occupied by Lady Betty. Lending support to the identification is the similarity of the room to known drawings of the interior which show the same windows on the left, the long vista into far rooms, as well as similar late seventeenth-century furnishings: the tapestry rug, Jacobean furniture and curtained, four-poster bed. Curiously, the paintings hung within the interior are less readily identifiable. Knole's collection is well-catalogued, but the paintings listed in Lady Betty's bedroom do not correspond precisely with the sketchy images in this painting. Hanging in the bedroom from 1839 to 1965 were *The Holy Family*, attributed to Anthony Van Dyck, *Judith with the Head of Holofernes* by Benvenuto Tisi Garofalo and various portraits of the Sackville family by Sir Godfrey Kneller. Two of the latter may be represented on the far wall. The heraldic design carved over the fireplace resembles the coat of arms of the Sackville family. The seascape as well as the Venetian scene to its right may represent paintings by the artist, since Holland executed marine and Italian views, but none is known to have been at Knole. Holland exhibited three views of Knole: two in 1845 at the British Institution and one in 1846 at the Royal Academy. He is best known as a watercolorist.

41. R. Huskisson (active 1832-54)
LORD NORTHWICK'S PICTURE GALLERY AT THIRLE-
STAINE HOUSE, GLOUCESTERSHIRE, ca. 1845-47

Oil on canvas, 23 x 42⅜ (81.3 x 107.7)
No. 1225
Coll: Lord Northwick; by descent to Captain E.G. Spencer-Churchill,
  Northwick Park: with Oscar and Peter Johnson from whom
  purchased 1968
Exh: The British Institution, 1847 (506) (?); Y.C.B.A. 1977 (87), repr.
Lit: *The Art Union*, 9 (March 1, 1847): 82; *A Catalogue of the Pictures, Works of
  Art etc. at Northwick Park*, 1864, reprint. 1908, p. 29, no. 203, as
  "Interior at Thirlestane House, Cheltenham"; Tancred Borenius,
  Catalogue of the Collection of Pictures at Northwick Park, 1921, p. 123,
  no. 309.

Thirlestaine House, located in Cheltenham, Gloucestershire,
housed about eight hundred of the paintings by Old Masters and
modern British painters which belonged to John, 2nd Baron Northwick (1770-1859). The remainder of the collection was housed at
Northwick Park, near Moreton-in-the Marsh.

The architect of Thirlestaine House was J.R. Scott, an amateur,
who began work in 1823. His use of the Grecian style, with Ionic
columns on the front portico, introduced neoclassicism to the growing resort area of Cheltenham. Wings were added on either side of
the house in the 1840s to serve as galleries for the art collection which
Lord Northwick opened to the public, and to whom he himself gave
guided tours. When Northwick died, the house was purchased by
Sir Thomas Phillips, who filled the galleries with books and manu-
scripts. In 1947 the house was bought by the neighboring Cheltenham
College and now serves as a dormitory as well as providing class-
rooms for the school (Simona Pakenham, *Cheltenham* [London,
1971], pp. 94, 112, 167-68).

The collection was described by Waagen, (*Treasures of Art in
Great Britain*, 3 [London, 1854]: 195ff.), who complained that its
quality was variable and that "pictures of the most various times and
schools are mingled together in the most arbitrary way." The present
view of the Dining Room, with a glimpse of the Salon and Ante-
room beyond, is evidence of Waagen's complaint. A number of
contemporary paintings can be identified, such as Francis Danby's
The Wood Nymph's Hymn to the Rising Sun (to the right of the door,
now in the Tate Gallery, London), purchased by Lord Northwick at

the R.A. of 1845, while Daniel Maclise's *Robin Hood and His Merry Men*, 1839, retouched in 1845, is at the extreme right above the sideboard. Such well known Old Masters as a copy of Titian's *Pope Paul III* (above the Danby) and Botticelli's *Portrait of a Young Man* (left of doorway, now in the National Gallery, London, then thought to be by Masaccio) can also be recognized.

The present painting was previously attributed to John Scarlett Davis, who died in 1845 after a long illness. G. Watkins Williams has suggested that the painting is by the little known Nottingham artist, R. Huskisson, and is that exhibited at the British Institution in 1847, a date supported by the presence of the Danby, painted in 1845.

42. Thomas Churchyard (1798–1865)
A HOUSE IN WOODBRIDGE, SUFFOLK, 1859

Signed, *Thos. Churchyard Woodbridge 1859*, lower right
Oil on panel, 7¼ x 10¾ (18.5 x 27.2)
B1976.7.98
Coll: G.R.D. Wallis; with Thos. Agnew & Sons from whom purchased
      1966

This early Victorian house, with its bow window fronting on the road, may still exist in Woodbridge, which is east of Ipswich, on the River Deben. Like many in the town, the house may have been constructed of the indigenous Suffolk yellow brick (see Michael Wright, "A Country Town in Good Heart," *CL* 163 [June 22, 1978]: 1816–18). Churchyard painted the house in the same year that the railroad came to Woodbridge. This transformed the town from a seaport to an expanding commercial center, and probably soon altered the rural countryside surrounding this house.

A lawyer and amateur artist, Churchyard lived in Woodbridge, where he painted this house and many local views and landscapes. He was an admirer of John Constable, also a Suffolk native, and painted with a fresh sense of color and rapid brush technique. One of Churchyard's friends wrote in 1847: "He will dash you off slight and careless sketches by the dozen, or score, but for touching and retouching, or finishing, that is quite another affair . . ." (D. Thomas, *Thomas Churchyard of Woodbridge* [Chislehurst, Kent, 1966], p. 8).

43. William Brown (1789–1859), attributed to
TIPTREE HALL AND FARM, ESSEX, ca. 1850–60

Oil on canvas, 20½ x 29½ (52 x 75)
No. 945
Coll: Thomas Laughton; sold Sotheby's March 18, 1964 (38); bt. P. & D.
    Colnaghi from whom purchased 1964

This painting shows the revival of the bird's-eye view which had gone out of favor in the eighteenth century. By the mid-nineteenth century technology and industrialization had become a new ideal in husbandry. Tiptree Farm was bought in a dilapidated state in 1841 by the agriculturalist John Mechi (1802–1880). In keeping with new interests, Mechi turned the farm into a modern productive business by using new methods of deep drainage and steam power (DNB). His book, *A Series of Letters on Agricultural Improvement* (London, 1845), contains a print of the farmstead as it was planned and first erected. The painting shows several differences, most noticeably in the addition of the garden and green-house to the left of the house. A second book published in 1857, *How to Farm Profitably* (London, 1857), explains how Mechi converted Tiptree into a model working farm. The painting probably dates from this period and shows the farm with all its modern accoutrements. It is still an active and productive farm today.

The painting is thought to be by William Brown, who executed two large panoramic bird's-eye views of the town of Louth, Lincolnshire, in 1847. They show the view of the village and countryside from the spire of Saint James Church and are now in the Town Hall in Louth. Brown planned to make engravings of these paintings along with a key to the houses depicted, and planned to sell them for one pound, five shillings. Such prints have not yet surfaced, so it is doubtful that the artist realized his money-making scheme (letter from L. Riddick, Town Clerk, Louth, July 5, 1978).

44. Nicholas Hawksmoor (1661–1736), attributed to
DESIGN FOR A BOWLING GREEN, HAMPTON COURT
PALACE, ca. 1689–92

Inscribed, verso, in brown ink, *Bowlingreen/ A Parterre of Ham/ =ton Court,*
    upper left
Pen and brown ink and grey wash, 14½ x 19⅞ (35.8 x 50.7)
B1975.2.377

The bowling green was an important part of the seventeenth-
century garden in England, and another elaborate example can be
seen in the view of Wollaton Hall (Cat. 3). The broad expanse of
lawn provided space not only for playing bowls, but also for promenading and viewing the garden as well. Samuel Pepys remarked in
his diary on July 22, 1666, after visiting France that:

> "the green of our bowling allis is better than any they have. So our
> business here being ayre, this is the best way, only with a little
> mixture of statues, or pots which may be handsome, and so filled
> with another pot of such or such flower or greene as the season of the
> year will bear."

The phrase "our being ayre" may refer to the fresh air, of which
Englishmen are traditionally fond.

Hawksmoor, the pupil of Vanburgh and one of England's
greatest Baroque architects, worked at Hampton Court Palace from
1689 to around 1691. According to Kerry Downes (*Hawksmoor*
[London, 1959], pp. 51–52, n. 9), no drawings by Hawksmoor are
known to survive of his work at Hampton Court, but the present
sheet may well be a candidate. The inscription appears to be early
and the drawing may be a genuine study rather than a copy.

45. Anonymous, XVII or XVIII Century
AN ORNAMENTAL POOL AND FOUNTAIN, ca. 1700

Brush and grey ink over pencil, (verso, red chalk study of male head)
    7⅜ x 10¾ (18.3 x 27)
B1977.14.6010

This drawing, formerly in the T.E. Lowinsky collection, shows a basin of water in an elaborate hillside garden inspired by Italian renaissance and seventeenth-century plans. It is similar in conception to the Neptune pool at the lowest area in the garden at Llannerch (Cat. 1). Fountains and basins of water, popular features of the seventeenth-century English garden, were recommended by John Worlidge in his *Systema Horticultura* (1677):

> "Fountains are Principal ornaments in a Garden, scarce a famous garden in Europe [is] without its fountain where primarily intended for batheing [sic] . . . The Italians bestow very great cost in Beautifying them for that use; the French are very prodigal in their Expenses about Fountains, and several curious gardens in England have them: but here only for ornament, they are generally made of stone, some square, others round or oval; and of divers other forms, some flat in the bottom, others round like a basin.

The style of drawing and type of garden represented may indicate a Dutch origin for this particular sheet.

46. British School, XVIII Century
DESIGN FOR A COUNTRY HOUSE, ca. 1700-1715

Pen and black ink and grey wash, 15 x 21⅜ (37.4 x 54)
B1975.2.628

This house design in the late Caroline or early Georgian style is reminiscent of early bird's-eye view paintings and engravings. The odd perspective, lack of background scenery, and strange details such as the small scale of the front gate indicate the work of a naive artist or architect working in the provinces. The coat of arms pasted in the upper right corner is related to the family of Fraser of Philorth and Lord Saltoun of Abernathy, Aberdeenshire. The motto above the crest: *Quam sibi sortem*, and below the shield: *en Dieu est tout* appears to be associated with Alexander Fraser, 12th Baron Saltoun (1654-1715), who may have commissioned the house and drawing. Harris 1979 (Cat. 174) suggests that the drawing is an unexecuted design for Philorth, Aberdeenshire, which burned down in the early twentieth century.

47. Leonard Knyff (1650-1722), attributed to
DESIGN FOR ORNAMENTAL GARDENS AND THE LONG
WATER AT HAMPTON COURT PALACE, ca. 1700-20

Pen, grey ink, watercolor and pencil, 6¼ x 19¾ (15.8 x 50)
B1977.14.6212

This view is thought to represent the garden at Hampton
Court as recreated in the geometric French and Dutch manner by the
garden architects George London and Henry Wise for William and
Mary, who came to the English throne in 1688. They brought with
them a continental taste for formality in garden planning. Three
straight walkways radiate out from the semicircular planting; the
parterre was probably planted with small hedges and knot gardens
(see Cat. 48). The wide *allées* are in accordance with the instructions
in John Parkinson's *Paradisi in Sole, Paradisus Terrestris* (1629), one of
the earliest and most popular garden books in England:

> "The fairer and larger your allées and walks be, the more grace your
> garden shall have, the less harm the herbs and flowers shall receive by
> passing by them that grow next unto the allée's sides, and the better
> shall your weeders cleanse both the beds and the allées."

The elaborate procession in the foreground may indicate that
the drawing was done for some commemorative print.

48. British School, XVIII Century
DESIGN FOR A KNOT GARDEN, BUSH HILL, 1713

Inscribed, recto, in brown ink, *a - Sand/ b Col[s]ash[er]/ c. ye Earth or=/
Border/ d Gravell/ e Col[s]ash[er]/ f ye long Bor:*, left margin; verso,
*Draught of a Knot for/ the Lower Quarter of/ The Long Garden at/
Bush=hill Drawn by Mr. Clarkes Gardiner 1713*
Pen, brown ink and watercolor over pencil, 9⅞ x 5⅝ (24.7 x 13.9)
B1975.3.362

The knot garden was a typical feature of the seventeenth-
century garden in England. The form was based on the continental
parterre which appeared in elaborate geometric shapes in France,
Italy, and the Netherlands. In this design, flowers and different

colors of sand and stone are placed in a swirling decorative pattern, and trees are cut into triangular topiary forms. A "broderie" area like this one designed by a gardener was meant to be viewed from above, perhaps from a terrace or banqueting house, so that it resembled a lush patterned carpet.

49. J. Slezer (d. 1714), ascribed to
THIRLESTANE CASTLE, NEAR LAUDER, VALE OF TWEED, ca. 1677

Inscribed, in brown ink, *Thirlestane Castle,* on scroll, upper edge
Pen and brown and grey ink (deeply shaded area of left tower has been
    patched on after original section was cut out), 10⅝ x 16⅞ (26.5 x 42.7)
B1975.2.616
Lit: Harris 1979 (Cat. 100).

Thirlestane Castle was built by John Lethington, Lord Thirlestane (1545-95) in 1590, to replace an older structure. The building was a long narrow block with a large round tower at each corner. These turrets were corbelled out to form a square top surmounted by gables. The Duke of Lauderdale (1616-82) enlarged the house and added wings to both sides. He also raised the terrace and placed the front door at that level. The drawing shows the house with these late seventeenth-century changes, and may have been taken from or intended for an engraving. The house is still standing today.

According to Harris (1979, Cat. 100), a north view of Thirlestane by Slezer, Jan Wyck and another was engraved ca. 1677. Slezer worked for the Lauderdales but very little is known about him.

50. Johannes Kip (1653-1722), after Leonard Knyff
LORD BURLINGTON'S HOUSE AT CHISWICK, ca. 1715

Inscribed in pen and brown ink, *The Thames,* on river, lower center
Engraving, 13⅜ x 19¼ (34.4 x 48.4)
B1977.14.18672

This engraving, executed by Kip after drawings or paintings by Knyff, is a loose plate from the popular folio size volumes entitled *Britannia Illustrata* (see Cat. 97). This bird's-eye view shows the extensive formal gardens at Chiswick, on the Thames above London. The prototype of such gardens was Versailles, designed by André Le

Nôtre for Louis XIV: a vast, geometrically ordered space surrounded by walkways in axial and radial patterns, parterres, straight canals, and small buildings. In a similar manner, the Chiswick gardens were an extension of the house and served as a series of outdoor rooms for parties as well as theatrical and musical presentations. Lord Burlington and William Kent later remodelled the garden in 1725 (Cat. 52), when they introduced curving paths, irregularly shaped canals, and classical temples and statuary to evoke an arcadian landscape.

51. Peter Tillemans (1684-1734), attributed to
VIEW OF THE HOUSE AND GARDEN AT UPPER WINCHENDEN, BUCKINGHAMSHIRE, ca. 1720-25

Inscribed, *Winchenden,* upper center
Watercolor, 13⅜ x 39⅞ (33.9 x 101.3) sight
No. 76/12/6/13

Winchenden was built by Philip, 4th Duke of Wharton (1613-95), around 1637, and was added to by his son Thomas and grandson Philip (d. 1731), who was created Duke of Wharton in 1718. The flat parterre garden in front of the house is typical of seventeenth-century formal landscaping, inspired in part by Louis XIV's Versailles. The building with long windows to the left of the main house was a green house, or orangery, where Thomas Wharton (noted for his oranges and vines) would have grown plants in tubs or large buckets. These were carried outside into the garden during the warmer months. An orangery is also visible in the foreground of Wollaton Hall (Cat. 3). The garden includes examples of topiary (trees and shrubs cut into geometric shapes), which became popular after the accession of William and Mary.

Formerly attributed to British School, the picture is now thought to be by Peter Tillemans, who came from Antwerp to England in 1708. He sketched around 500 drawings for John Bridges's *History of Northampton* (London, ?1739), painted similar views, such as *Livermere Park* (Oscar and Peter Johnson) and specialized in sporting paintings. While working at Newmarket, he may have met the Duke of Wharton, a horse racing enthusiast. This watercolor is probably the preparatory design for Tillemans's oil painting of the same scene in a less horizontal format (25¼ x 35½, Private Collection, England). The oil represents the house from an identical viewpoint but includes several figures, the Duke, and a liveried servant in the foreground. Harris 1979 (Cats. 149 and 149b) does not mention attribution to Tilleman of either the oil or the preparatory sketch.

52. William Kent (1685-1748)
DESIGN FOR A SCREEN AND GATEWAY AT CHISWICK, ca. 1725-30

Pen, black ink and brown and grey wash over pencil, 10½ x 14⅞
   (26.5 x 37.3)
B1975.2.151

William Kent, apprenticed in his native Yorkshire to a local sign and coach painter, left his position at a young age and went to London and then on to Rome. He spent about ten years in Italy reproducing Old Masters for aristocratic patrons in England. While there, he became friendly with Lord Burlington, a young nobleman interested in architecture, with whom he was to collaborate on several buildings. Burlington introduced Kent to landscape design and encourage him to create new gardens for his house at Chiswick (see Cat. 50). This design for a gateway probably dates from 1725-30 when the house and garden were under construction. The structure was perhaps intended to stand at the entrance to the garden, where it would screen the view from the visitor until he stepped through it into the landscape.

53. William Kent (1685-1748)
DESIGN FOR A DEER PARK, ca. 1730s

Pen and brush and brown ink, 6⅝ x 11⅝ (16.6 x 29.3)
B1975.2.617

Horace Walpole wrote that William Kent "leaped the fence and saw that all nature was a garden." Here, nature and animals are incorporated into a scene of lush grazing land and thickly wooded areas. A sunken ditch or "Ha-Ha" usually separated livestock from the garden area and provided a seemingly endless vista without the intrusion of a visible fence. The deer house with its conical roof (right background) served as a garden "folly," a structure at the termination of a vista to catch and hold the viewer's eye and imagination.

54. William Kent (1685-1748)
TEMPLE DESIGN FOR SHOTOVER PARK, OXFORDSHIRE,
ca. 1738-45

Inscribed, verso, in brown ink, probably by the artist, *W.K.*, center; in black
  ink, *Coll: Tyerrell/ in Oxfordshire*, upper center
Pen, black ink and brown wash over pencil, 11⅛ x 12⅜ (28.4 x 31)
B1975.2.152

Kent worked at Rousham, near Shotover Park, from 1738 to
1740. He probably worked at Shotover at the same time or soon after
finishing the famous landscape at Rousham. This classical temple
design, probably derived from a pattern book or an actual building
Kent had seen in Italy, was set on a mound to the south of the
Wilderness garden from where it commanded a vista above the
radiating walkways at Shotover. Mrs. Powys visited the garden in
1769 and wrote:

> "It is within four miles of Oxford, a magnificent place, an elegant
> stone house which stands in the centre of very fine gardens . . .
> straight avenues terminated by obelisks, temples, porticoes, etc.; it
> has an air of grandeur."

55. British School, XVIII Century
PLAN OF THE PARK AT NORTON HALL, ca. 1750-60

Inscribed, in pen and brown ink, *A. Norton Hall/ B, The Large Sheet of water
  supplyd/ from ye. Well, CC. The Farmhouse opposite/ the great C[?r]ime.
  DD. The two pleasure Woods/ E. The fountain well supplying by/ Pipes
  the Family at Norton & Bath/ in the Wood/ F The strict Course of the Canal
  as limited by the act/ G The course of taking the/ canal to ye Hempstones as
  lst pro=/ pos'd by ye act 2 Geo 2nd . . . which would avoid the present
  alterations. H. The tract the Duke is now aim/ing to go leading thro' Sir
  Richard's/ pleasure woods & Lawns & spring between/ the fountain well,
  Hall & large sheet Well*, on scroll at lower edge
Pen and black ink and grey wash, 9¾ x 14⅜ (24.4 x 36.2)
B1975.2.35

The drawing may have been produced by a surveyor to chart
a dispute over the line of a canal. The Duke seemed to want to take
his canal right through Sir Richard's "pleasure woods." It also
shows, however, a typical parkland in the manner of Lancelot
"Capability" Brown. Trees are planted at irregular intervals, either
singly or in small clumps. A classical temple, a bridge in the Chinese
style, and other follies are scattered about the property, and the lake

is designed in serpentine curves. The house is in the severely classical
Palladian style.

56. John Sanderson (d. 1774), attributed to
ELEVATION OF AN UNKNOWN COUNTRY HOUSE, ca.
1750-60

Pen, black ink and grey wash, with touches of brown wash, 10¾ x 17⅝
    (26.7 x 44.5)
B1975.2.345

The architect Colen Campbell popularized this type of
Palladian house in his *Vitruvius Britannicus* (Cat. 98). His own
designs for Wanstead House, Essex (Cat. 81), Houghton Hall,
Norfolk (1722), and Stourhead, Wiltshire (ca. 1721), with their
temple fronts and rusticated ground floors provided inspiration for
numerous architects and country house builders. This design is
similar to Campbell's plan for Lord Herbert's house in Whitehall,
London (ca. 1723-24, now demolished), which also had a temple
front with pilasters at either end, central columns *in antis,* and arches
cut into the rusticated ground floor. Little is known about the
architect, John Sanderson, except that he was the cousin of Joseph
Sanderson, who designed renovations for Okeover Hall, Staffordshire, which is also shown in this exhibition (Cat. 15).

57. John Sanderson (d. 1774), attributed to
PLAN FOR AN UNKNOWN COUNTRY HOUSE, ca. 1750-60

Pen, black ink, grey and brown wash, 14¼ x 19¾ (36 x 49.8)
B1975.2.348

This plan shows the interior for the Palladian style house
attributed to Sanderson (Cat. 56). The facade shown in the elevation
is at the top of this plan where the columns and pilasters are clearly
visible. The house is arranged around a central hall: a thirty-six foot
"Cube Room." This impressive high-ceilinged space would serve as
a reception room for guests. The room to the right with an apse at
one end may have been the dining room. Across the cube room are
two smaller areas, perhaps for more intimate dining or conversation.
Upon entering, the visitor could easily walk on a straight axis from
the front of the house to the garden side where a balustraded terrace
provided a view of the landscape.

58. John Baptist Claude Chatelain (ca. 1710–ca. 1771)
A VIEW OF THE ROTUNDA IN THE GARDEN AT STOWE,
BUCKINGHAMSHIRE, 1753

Pencil and brown and grey washes, incised for transfer, 9⅛ x 12⅞
   (23.1 x 32.4)
B1975.4.1058

The garden at Stowe was one of the most famous of its time.
Richard Temple, Viscount Cobham, began reconstructing the space
with Charles Bridgeman in 1710. William Kent transformed it into a
classical Arcadia in the 1730s with the addition of the Elysian Fields
and a Grecian Valley. He supervised the building of and perhaps
designed the Rotunda, the Temples of Venus and Contemplation,
and to supplement his literary ideas, added a Temple of Ancient
Virtue and a Temple of the British Worthies with busts by Rysbrack
and his studio. As head gardener here in 1741, Capability Brown cut
sweeping cross views through the avenues and added the grotto as
well as more temples. His work at Stowe was well received and he
went on after 1748 to numerous commissions for important gardens
such as those at Warwick Castle (Cat. 22).

Chatelain's drawing is one of a series of views at Stowe which
were engraved in 1753 by George Bickham, Jr. (d. 1758) as *Sixteen
Perspective Views, Together with a General Plan of the Magnificent
Buildings at Stow* [sic]. A French artist, active as a drawing master in
England, Chatelain specialized in views of gardens and landscapes.
His method of using bodycolor (or gouache) influenced Paul Sandby
(Cat. 61).

59. British School, XVIII Century
HAWKSTONE HALL, SHROPSHIRE, ca. 1760–70

Pencil, pen and ink, watercolor and pastel on paper backed with linen,
   13⅜ x 19¼ (33.6 x 49)
B1975.2.624

Hawkstone Hall, near Weston in north Shropshire, as seen in
this view had been built over two periods. The original house, the
three-bay central area with a temple front, was built for Sir Richard
Hill around 1720. The portico extends one and a half stories and
there are small blocked square windows just beneath the pediment.
The wings were added by Sir Rowland Hill, Richard's nephew,

around 1750 to make the house a larger and more impressive building. The resulting nine-bay red-brick structure, with stone quoining and decorative features, is now a College of the Order of the Redemptionists. The watercolor was formerly attributed to John Russell, R.A. (1745-1806). The name of Thomas Malton, the Elder (1726-1801) has also been suggested.

60. James Stuart (1713-88), attributed to
DECORATION FOR A DINING ROOM, ca. 1760s

Inscribed, in black ink, 25—°/ 30-..°, in oval, center; and with other
    dimensions
Pen and black ink over pencil, and grey wash with touches of blue,
    27¼ x 19⅛ (69 x 48.2)
B1975.2.344

James "Athenian" Stuart was a leading figure in the neoclassical movement. In 1751, he and Nicholas Revett made an expedition to Greece where they executed measured drawings of ancient monuments. These were published in 1762 as *The Antiquities of Athens,* and had a great impact on the architectural taste of the period. Stuart was also successful as an architect and decorator. His interior designs for Kedleston, Derbyshire of 1757 are among the earliest to show both the architectural features and the placement of furniture in the rooms. The present design is an example of a working drawing for a room which would allow both architect and client to visualize the arrangement of the room, its decorative plaster-work, sculpture in niches and structural elements. The corners have been cut out so that the walls of the room may be folded up to simulate the actual space to be constructed.

61. Paul Sandby, R.A. (1730-1809)
VIEW OF WAKEFIELD LODGE IN WHITTLEBURY FOREST, NORTHAMPTONSHIRE, 1767

Signed, in gold, *P. Sandby 1767,* lower left
Pen and black ink with watercolor over pencil, 16⅝ x 33⅜ (42.3 x 84.9)
B1977.14.4648

Wakefield Lodge was designed as a large hunting lodge for the 2d Duke of Grafton, who may be represented with the group in the left foreground. William Kent designed the lodge with its Tuscan portico and lunette windows. Work was incomplete at the time of

74

Kent's death in 1748, and Capability Brown probably completed the landscape setting. The lodge stands on a hill overlooking an ornamental lake. For further details on the watercolor, see Christopher White, *English Landscape, 1630-1850* (Yale Center for British Art, 1977, Cat. 37).

Sandby was trained as a draftsman and worked for the Military Drawing Office in London. His experiments with the etching process led to the popularization of the aquatint technique. He also worked extensively with watercolors and contributed to the development of the medium (formerly used primarily to color engravings) as a form of pictorial expression. He was a founding member of the Royal Academy.

62. Thomas Beilby (ca. 1740-ca. 1819)
CHATSWORTH, DERBYSHIRE, 1774

Inscribed, in black ink, *Chatsworth the Seat of his Grace the Duke of Devonshire,* lower center; *Fec't June 1774,* lower right
Watercolor with pen and ink, 4⅜ x 7⅛ (11.1 x 18.1)
B1977.14.1356-1406,fol.19

This postcard-size sketch book has forty-six meticulously finished watercolor drawings and five uncolored drawings of buildings and scenery in Yorkshire and the Midlands. There is a manuscript index written by Beilby, a native of Yorkshire, listing all the places portrayed and inscribed inside the front cover is: *DRAWINGS after NATURE/ By/ Thos. Beilby Sheffield York:sr 1775.*

This view shows the south and west fronts of Chatsworth, one of the most famous of all country houses. The original Tudor house, built by Sir William Cavendish in the 1550s, was slowly remodelled by the 3rd Earl, later 1st Duke of Devonshire. He engaged William Talman (1650-1719) to design and remodel the house. The architect's south front, completed in 1686 and the most baroque of the four facades, incorporated applied pilasters, large keystones over the windows, and a balustrade with urns across the top of the building. By 1774, when this view was painted, Capability Brown had improved the landscape by clearing away unobstructed views of the River Derwent and had moved the bridge (center) to its present location. The Duke had also moved the entire neighboring village of Chatsworth to another locale so that his view of the Derbyshire terrain would appear in its natural state. For another view of Chatsworth see Cat. 88.

63. Robert Adam (1728-1792)
A CASTELLATED COUNTRY HOUSE IN A LANDSCAPE,
ca. 1775-85

Pencil and watercolor, with pen and black ink, on three sheets of joined
paper, 12 x 18⅝ (30 x 47)
B1975.2.149

Adam's design for a medieval manor house, with its asymmetrical, crenellated facade and round towers, may have been proposed as the preliminary idea for an actual commission. The architect executed many compositions of imaginary castles in wild landscapes during the 1780s, perhaps influenced by the work of Alexander Cozens and William Gilpin, whose *Tours* was published in 1783. But these picturesque drawings were never intended as building projects. In this example, however, Adam's linear rendering of the castle on the central strip of paper is not only meticulously detailed, but also pictorially independent of its rural setting. Adam may have drawn up the plan for a client and then later decided to incorporate it into a landscape by pasting additional strips of paper to the upper and lower edges. It is more simple and severe than Adam's castellated country houses, such as Culzean, designed by 1777 for the Earl of Cassilis, Ayrshire, Scotland.

Adam is best known as the architect of several monumental houses such as Kedleston, Derbyshire (ca. 1761), and for his airy, neoclassical interiors such as those at Syon House, Middlesex (ca. 1762).

64. William E. Emes (d. 1803)
GARDEN DESIGN FOR NORTHWICH PARK, 1778

Inscribed, in black ink, *A PLAN of the Intended Alterations/ Immediately about
the House at/ NORTHWICH/ the Seat of/ Sir John Rushout Bart./ By
Wm. Emes/ 1778,* upper left; and with other identifications in ink and
pencil; inscribed verso, in brown ink, *R Northwick Sketch for Improvement of Northwick-Park/By Mr Emes-/1778*
Pen and black ink and pencil on two sheets of joined paper, 17¼ x 25½
(43.8 x 63.7)
B1975.2.350

This plan for a late eighteenth-century garden indicates the movement away from the pictureque and allusive garden designs at

Stowe, Stourhead and Rousham toward the more open and natural spaces envisioned by Capability Brown. The simple, almost stark landscape sweeps directly up to the house. The garden was intended to extend as far as the eye could see and to flow into the surrounding countryside. A Ha-Ha, the "sunk Fence that divides the Park from the Sheep Pasture," was used for this purpose. Temples, fountains, and garden follies are conspicuously absent. Banks of trees are used to mask buildings, such as the Keeper's Lodge at the lower left, and the kitchen and fruit gardens are hidden behind "A Shrubbery." The presence of a Hot House is indicative of the growing interest in new species of plants and flowering trees. A refinement of the orangery, as seen at Wollaton Hall (Cat. 3) and the Earl of Rochester's house (Cat. 9), the Hot House was to be further transformed into a building entirely of glass, as at Tiptree Hall Farm (Cat. 43) and in George Shepherd's watercolor of an unknown house (Cat. 87).

Emes was a resident land surveyor at Elvetham Park, Hampshire. His son John (d. ca. 1810) was an artist and engraver.

65. Moses Griffith (1747–after 1809)
BEVERE HOUSE, NEAR NORTH CLAINES, WORCESTERSHIRE, ca. 1780

Inscribed, in pencil, *Bevere D. Nash's Worcestershire,* lower center
Pencil and watercolor, with pen and black ink, 13⅝ x 19⅜ (34.4 x 48.8)
B1975.2.163

The artist represents Bevere, built for Anthony Keck around 1750, as a typical mid-eighteenth century brick house with a porch of four Ionic columns, a Venetian window over it, and above, a tripartite lunette window. The inscription *D. Nash's Worcestershire* may indicate that the picture was intended as an illustration to the historian's *Collections for the History of Worcestershire* (2 vols., London, 1781–82). The author is identified as Treadway Russell Nash, who, according to Pevsner, lived at Bevere House.

Moses Griffith spent most of his artistic career working for Thomas Pennant and his son David, of Nantleys, St. Asaph, Flintshire, in north Wales. The Welsh born artist travelled with the Pennants and made sketches and watercolors for them. This view, which once belonged to the elder Pennant, may date to a sketching journey that Griffith made in 1780 to the neighboring county of

Staffordshire. A self-taught artist, Griffith was strongly influenced by Paul Sandby (Cat. 61) and his work has a fresh and charming naiveté.

66. British School, XVIII Century, after Thomas Hearne (1744-1806)
HEVENINGHAM HALL, SUFFOLK, ca 1782-90

Inscribed, in pencil, verso, *Blenheim Duke of Marlborough's House*
Watercolor, 6½ x 10¼ (17.4 x 25.5)
B1977.14.1146

The inscription on the back of the drawing is erroneous. Heveningham, a large Palladian house, was designed by Sir Robert Taylor (1714-88), an architect who belonged to the Burlington school. It was built for Sir Gerard Vanneck and the construction was completed by the architect James Wyatt around 1788. Wyatt designed the interior in the neoclassical style of Robert Adam. The grand house is sited on top of a hill to command an encompassing view of the gently rolling terrain.

In 1780, Thomas Hearne executed a larger watercolor of Heveningham, nearly identical to this one (Mrs. Tighe-Wood Collection), which was engraved by William Watts for his *Seats of the Nobility and Gentry* (London, 1779-86). The print includes a foreground group with horses, two male figures near the river and the coach drawn by four horses in the middle distance, all of which are omitted in the present drawing. It was formerly attributed to Hearne, but is now believed to be a copy by an unknown artist after the print.

67. [?T] Sanders
SUNDORNE CASTLE, NEAR SHREWSBURY, SHROP-SHIRE, 1783

Inscribed, in ink, *Sundorne/ [?T.] Sanders-Salop 1783,* lower right
Pen and brush and grey ink and pencil, 10¼ x 16 (26 x 40.3)
B1975.2.615

This view shows the house as it was originally built in the early eighteenth century in the Georgian style. According to Pevsner, the house was reconstructed with a castellated symmetrical facade in the early nineteenth century. It was demolished after 1958. The bare sweep of lawn punctuated by a single tree or tightly bunched clumps of trees, with unobstructed views toward a body of water, is typical

78

of the influence of Capability Brown. Sanders may have been a local amateur artist from Shrewsbury or as it is sometimes written, 'Salop'.

68. Joseph Farington, R.A. (1747-1821)
PATTERDALE PALACE, WESTMORLAND, ca. 1790

Watercolor, pen and ink, and pencil, 8¼ x 13⅝ (21 x 34.3)
B1977.14. 1853-1896, fol. 20

Patterdale, a village at the head of Ullswater Lake, was known as one of the most picturesque places in the Lake district. This house and its owner was described by William Gilpin in his *Observations relative chiefly to the Picturesque Beauties* (Vol 2, London, 1786):

> "Over the cottages of this village, there is a house belonging to a person of somewhat better condition; whose little estate lies in the neighbourhood. As his property, inconsiderable as it is, is better than that of any of his neighbors, it has gained him the title of King of Patterdale, of which his family name is lost. His ancestors have long enjoyed the title before him. We had the honor of seeing the prince . . . I could not help thinking that if I were inclined to envy the situation of any potentate in Europe, it would be that of the King of Patterdale. The pride of Windsor and Versailles would shrink in a comparison with the magnificence of his dominions."

This view of the Palace of Patterdale, bound in a leather sketchbook labelled GRAY'S JOURNAL, is one of forty-three drawings of the Lake District executed by Farington. Farington, a landscape painter best known for his *Diary,* was born at Leigh, Lancashire, and studied with Richard Wilson (Cat. 20). He was one of the first students at the Royal Academy and exhibited regularly there from 1778-1813. May of his views of the Lakes were engraved.

69. British School, XVIII Century
VIEW OF AN UNIDENTIFIED GEORGIAN HOUSE, ca. 1790

Watercolor with pen and black ink, 15⅞ x 31 (40.3 x 78.7)
B1977.14.6277

This elaborately detailed view of a porticoed Georgian house was formerly attributed to Thomas Sandby, R.A. (1721-98). It appears to be an "office" drawing, however, as an imaginary or preliminary idea from an architect. The style of the house is reminiscent of the work of William Chambers (1723-96) or James Paine (ca. 1716-89). The landscape may have been added by another hand.

70. Humphrey Repton (1752-1818)
STUDY FOR AN ILLUSTRATION IN "SKETCHES AND HINTS ON LANSCAPE GARDENING," 1794

Inscribed in brown ink, *Studies in Landscape Gardening*, lower center
Brush, grey and yellow wash over pencil, 6½ x 10⅝ (16.4 x 27)
B1977.14.9505

In *Sketches and Hints on Landscape Gardening* (1794), Repton advocated the use of "trees of a pointed or conic shape" with classical or Grecian buildings. He believed that evergreens provide a good contrast to the curved forms of the buildings because they recall the Italian landscapes of Claude and Poussin, where "we see Grecian edifices blended with firs and cypresses." The lines of Gothic buildings should be contrasted with deciduous or "round-headed" trees because fir trees would compete with the spires of the architecture. This double image, illustrated as Plate 7 in Repton's book, proves the point to the reader by allowing him to see the various possibilities. The classical house to the left stands in a group of deciduous trees; beneath the flap is the more appropriate setting for a Gothic house amidst such trees. On the right side beneath the flap is the classical building in a dramatic setting of fir trees.

71. Jonathan Fisher (ca. 1760-1809)
A SUMMERHOUSE IN THE RUSTIC STYLE, 1795

Inscribed, in pencil, *J. Fisher 1795*, on mat, lower right
Watercolor over pencil, 8½ x 12⅛ (21.2 x 30.4)
B1975.4.1180

The "rustic" was a popular style for occasional garden architecture, used as an alternative to classically based garden follies, castellated sham facades, or fake ruins. Similar buildings were sometimes intended as hermitages where a man was paid by the owner of the garden to add verisimilitude to the idea of a contemplative retreat. The gardens at Stowe and Stourhead had hermitages, but it proved difficult to find men with the pure hermit or monastic temperament to live in them. Thatched cottages such as this example reflected the influence of the French theoretician, Abbé Marc-Antoine Laugier (1711-69), whose *Essai sur l'architecture* (1753) advocated a return to primitive or natural forms of architecture as expressions of a pastoral ideal.

Fisher was born in Dublin and was a self-taught artist. In 1782, he published a set of views of the Lake of Killarney and Irish scenery aquatinted after his paintings. He exhibited in Dublin throughout his life.

72. Joseph Mallord William Turner, R.A. (1775-1851)
A THREE STORIED GEORGIAN HOUSE IN A PARK, ca. 1795

Pencil, grey and blue wash, 4⅜ x 10⅞ (11.1 x 27.6)
B1977.14.5603

The present drawing of an unknown house is one of many in the style of Dr. Monro's circle executed ca. 1795.

73. James Wyatt, R.A. (1746-1813), and J.M.W. Turner, R.A. (1775-1851)
A PROJECTED DESIGN FOR FONTHILL ABBEY, WILTSHIRE, 1798

Inscribed on a contemporary label on the backboard, *North West View of a Building/ Erecting at Fonthill in Wiltshire/ the Seat of Wm. Beckford Esq/ in the Style of a Gothic Abbey/ James Wyatt. R.A.*
Watercolor on paper backed with linen, 26⅜ x 41½ (67 x 105.4)
B1975.4.1880

This drawing is a finished presentation drawing, exhibited at the Royal Academy in 1798 (955). It commemorates an example of Wyatt's work for William Beckford (1760-1844) between 1796-1812. The octagonal tower shown here, however, ending in a spire supported by eight flying buttresses, was never built. Beckford continuously changed his mind both before and during the actual construction of the increasingly elaborate structure and Wyatt was not always diligent. Fonthill Abbey was the most extravagant expression of picturesque Gothic revivalism in the early nineteenth century. Beckford retired to Bath in 1822 and in 1825, the poorly-constructed, second octagonal tower of Fonthill collapsed, demolishing much of the house. (See Harris 1979, Cat. 395).

Wyatt was a prolific architect who worked in a number of

styles (see Cats. 32 and 76), and it seems that Turner was used in this example to paint the background. The style of the background looks convincing and it says much for Turner's professional attitude that he would be willing to perform such tasks, although he had been happy enough to wash in the background of architects' drawings at the outset of his career, ten years earlier.

74. Thomas Girtin (1775-1802)
HAREWOOD HOUSE, YORKSHIRE, ca. 1798

Inscribed, in pencil, *Harewood,* lower center
Pencil, 7⅜ x 14¼ (18.5 x 36)
B1975.3.1192

This Palladian house was built from 1759 to 1771 for Edwin Lascelles, who was created Baron Harewood in 1790. The architectural design for it by John Carr of York appears in Colen Campbell's *Vitruvius Britannicus,* Vol. 5 (see Cat. 98). Robert Adam designed the interiors (1759-71), and in 1843, Sir Charles Barry was to add another story to the pavilion wings and put massive Corinthian balustrades around the roof. He also replaced the landscape garden (see Cat. 75) with a formal terraced area in the Italian sixteenth- or seventeenth-century manner.

Girtin spent much time in the last years of his life at Harewood, where Lord Harewood maintained a room for him. The artist executed several large finished watercolors of the house and this drawing may have served as a preliminary idea for one of them. During his brief life, Girtin had many other notable patrons for his watercolors, including the Earl of Elgin, the Earl of Essex, Lord Mulgrave and Sir George Beaumont. Born in London, he was apprenticed to Edward Dayes in 1789. There he met J.M.W. Turner and both men were strongly influenced by Dayes's style and method.

75. Thomas Girtin (1775-1802)
A TEMPLE IN HAREWOOD PARK, ca. 1798

Watercolor and pencil, 11⅞ x 11 (30.4 x 27.6)
B1975.3.1193

The garden at Harewood was created by Capability Brown around 1772 to complement the recently completed house (Cat. 74).

Brown enlarged the lake, planted great numbers of trees, and exploited the expansive rolling hills and green fertile countryside to create a typical English landscape park. He erected garden follies and temples, such as this example, to serve as termination points for vistas, as well as places to rest during a tour of the garden. Girtin's view was sketched from below and behind the temple, which is partially hidden by a copse of trees.

76. James Wyatt, R.A. 1747-1813), attributed to
PROJECT FOR AN UNIDENTIFIED COUNTRY HOUSE, ca. 1800

Watercolor and pencil, with pen and black ink, 20½ x 29½ (52 x 74.5)
B1975.2.357

James Wyatt was an eclectic architect whose style varied according to the dictates of fashion or his patrons, so that he was equally able to produce Gothic designs, such as at Lee Priory or Fonthill (Cats. 32 and 76), or to work in a neoclassical style as in this example.

77. British School, XIX Century
OLD HOUSE AT FONTHILL, WILTSHIRE, ca. 1800-1810

Inscribed, in brown ink, *Old House. Fonthill. Wilts/ copied from a painting at the Abbey,* lower left; in pencil, *Height 5.4. Length 6.6.* along left margin
Watercolor and pencil, with subsidiary sketch in pencil in lower half of sheet, 9 x 9 (22.6 x 22.6)
B1975.2.25

This view shows Fonthill Splendens, the Palladian house completed in 1768 for Alderman William Beckford (1709-70). It was set in a landscape park with grottoes and lakes. The owner's son, William Beckford (1760-1844), reacting against the classical Palladian mode, built his extravagant Fonthill Abbey nearby in the Gothic style (Cat. 73).

The artist of the drawing made a grid on the paper to facilitate the transfer of the design, presumably from a larger painting hanging at Fonthill to this smaller drawing. The pencil sketch in the lower half is a close-up, detailed elevation of the house, which is no longer extant.

78. Joseph Mallord William Turner, R.A. (1775-1851)
A VIEW OF HAMPTON COURT, HEREFORDSHIRE, FROM
THE NORTHWEST, 1806

Pen, ink and watercolor over black lead, 7^{15}/$_{16}$ x 11 ^{15}/$_{16}$ (20.2 x 30.3)
B1975.4.1766

      Turner had visted Hampton Court in 1795 when he made
pencil sketches in the *South Wales* sketchbook (A.J. Finberg, *A
Complete Inventory of the Drawings of the Turner Bequest,* London,
1909, XXVI, fo. 51, 52 and 53). There are further drawings in the
Hereford Court sketchbook of 1798 (Finberg, *op. cit.,* XXXVIII,
folio 66 and 67). Finished watercolors were produced from slightly
differing viewpoints and are now at the Whitworth Art Gallery,
University of Manchester (see Sabin Exhibition, 1973 (11-14). This
and the following watercolor were commissioned by Sir Richard
Colt Hoare in 1806 as illustrations for his copy of Thomas Earl of
Coningsby's private publication of *An Account of the Manor of Marden
in Hertfordshire* (1722-25). The correspondence between Turner and
Colt Hoare concerning the commission, (1805-1806), was published
by Kenneth Woodbridge (*Landscape and Antiquity,* 1970, pp. 172,
182-83).

      The viewpoint chosen is similar to f. 53 in the *South Wales*
sketchbook and records alterations to Hampton Court by Viscount
Malden, for which he may have employed James Wyatt (see Cornforth, 1973; see Cats. 4, 5 and 6 for a more detailed history of
Hampton Court).

79. Joseph Mallord William Turner, R.A. (1775-1851)
A VIEW OF HAMPTON COURT, HEREFORDSHIRE, FROM
THE SOUTHEAST, 1806

Pen, ink and watercolor over black lead, 7^{15}/$_{16}$ x 11^{15}/$_{16}$ (20.2 x 30.3)
B1975.4.1765

      See previous entry. The original pencil drawing for the present
watercolor appears on page 51 of the *South Wales* sketchbook of
1795. An engraving after Turner by J. Walker was published in the
Copper-Plate Magazine (1797), taken from an almost identical viewpoint.

80. Samuel Davis (1756-1819)
RIVER SCENE WITH AN UNIDENTIFIED COUNTRY
HOUSE, ca. 1806-18

Watercolor and pencil, 10½ x 16 (26.4 x 40.4)
B1977.14.157

    This view shows a Palladian country house with a four-columned portico which is sited on the side of a hill to take advantage of the view toward the river below. The configuration of the terrain may represent the Thames valley above Reading.

    Samuel Davis was born in the West Indies and grew up in England. He travelled to India as a young man, became the Accountant General for Bengal and sketched the local buildings and countryside. His style resembles that of Thomas Daniell, an artist with whom he may have studied in India. Davis returned to England in 1806 at the age of fifty and thereafter executed many watercolors of landscapes and country houses. As demonstrated by this view, the artist was more interested in representing pure landscape than the architectural details of the house.

81. Rev. Thomas Streatfeild (1777-1848)
WANSTEAD HOUSE, ESSEX, 1807

Inscribed, probably by the artist, in brown ink, *Wanstead. 1807,* lower center
Watercolor with pen and brown ink, 6 x 8⅝ (15.2 x 21.6)
B1975.2.6

    Wanstead was built by Colen Campbell for Sir Richard Child, later Earl Tylney, from 1715-1720. Campbell, the author of *Vitruvius Britannicus* (Cat. 98), claimed that this Palladian building with its large hexastyle, six-columned portico (visible here from the side) was the first of its type in England. The block-like building with little or no architectural ornament, derived from the designs of Palladio and Inigo Jones, became a popular form of domestic architecture in England during the eighteenth century. The artist specialized in topographical views and painted a series of castles, some engraved in *Copperplate Magazine.* He spent much of his life collecting material for a history of Kent.

82. Lewis Kennedy
FLOWER GARDEN AT MIDDLETON PARK, OXFORD-
SHIRE, 1811

Inscribed, in black ink, *Plan/ for a/ Flower-Garden &/ at/ Middleton Park/ The
seat of the Rt. Hon.able. the Earl of Jersey/ Proposed by/ his obedient
servant/ Lewis Kennedy/ Hammersmith Sept. 19. 1811,* upper left
Pen and brush, and grey ink touched with pencil, 19¼ x 24⅝ (48.8 x 62.2)
B1975.2.208

Kennedy's plan demonstrates the influence of Humphrey
Repton and John Claudius Loudon (1783-1843) on landscape design
in the nineteenth century. Loudon, who wrote several didactic
books such as *The Encyclopedia of Gardening* (1822) and the eight-
volume *Arboretum et Fruticetum Britannicum* (1833-38), inspired
innovations in horticulture and gardening within structured spaces.
Loudon's ideal garden was based on a lawn scattered with comma-
shaped flower beds similar to these abundant examples at Middleton.
Both Loudon and Repton advocated the planting of rare and exotic
varieties of flowers which were intended to be seen individually, and
they placed trees in clumps or in bands at the edges of the garden.
Also typical of the new taste in landscape is George Shepherd's
watercolor of an unidentified house and conservatory (Cat. 87).

At the time of this drawing, the owner of Middleton (usually
known as Middleton Stoney) was George Villiers, Earl of Jersey
(1773-1859).

83. John Claude Nattes (1765-1822)
BILLIARD ROOM AT WOLSINGTON, NORTHUMBER-
LAND, 1811

Inscribed, in brown ink, *July 2/1811 Interior of the Billiard Room at Woolsington
[sic],* lower left
Watercolor and pencil, 9⅛ x 12⅞ (23.1 x 32.8)
B1977.14.3308

The game of billiards became fashionable for both men and
women in the late eighteenth and early nineteenth centuries. The
tables were often placed in bay windows or in extensions of larger
rooms. This room appears to be an old orangery with French windows on the left presumably opening out to the garden on the south
side of the house.

This is one of forty-seven drawings in a sketchbook which is inscribed on its cover: *47/ Drawings from Nature/ by J.C. Nattes/ 1811./ Wolsington & &, Northumberland/ Ferney Hill, Kelso, Melrose & &/ Roxburghshire, N.B.*. Nattes was a watercolorist who published sketches from his tours in *Scotia Depicta* (1804) and *Select Views of Bath, Bristol, Malvern, Cheltenham, and Weymouth* (1805). He was one of the founding members of the Watercolour Society in 1804, and exhibited frequently with the Royal Academy.

84. James Ward (1769-1859)
OLD HALL, TABLEY, CHESHIRE, 1814 or 1819

Inscribed in pencil, *J.W. Old Hall. Table[y] /July 20th. 181[?4 or 9]*, lower right
Pencil, 5⅞ x 14⅛ (10.6 x 30.4)
B1977.14.4217

The Old Hall stood on an island in Nether Tabley Lake, near Knutsford. The castellated structure, built around 1380, was a three-story square block building. It was not torn down when the new Georgian house was built for Sir Peter Leicester in 1762-69. The building became a ruin and was the subject of this romantic yet topographically accurate view by Ward. The artist visited Tabley often and did many sketches and paintings there, such as *Cattle at a Pool at Sunrise, Tabley* (Cat. 38). The most famous views of Tabley were painted by Turner.

85. John Sell Cotman (1782-1842)
RAYNHAM HALL, NORFOLK, ca. 1818-19

Signed, in pencil, *J.S. Cotman 18[   ]*, lower right
Pencil and grey wash, 6⅜ x 11¼ (16.2 x 28.6)
B1975.2.531

Raynham was built for Sir Roger Townshend, a Norfolk landowner interested in architecture, who travelled to the continent to get ideas for his house. The house was begun in 1635 and incorporates gables with curving sides and volutes in the Dutch style common in East Anglia and similar to those on the house at Llannerch (Cat. 1). The architect was also influenced by Inigo Jones, as indicated by the narrow, Ionic portico on the east facade. Raynham was an innovative house for its period. It was altered by William Kent in the eighteenth century to present a more classicizing appearance in the manner of Inigo Jones.

A later hand has inscribed on the mat "Engraved for Excursion May 1, 1819," suggesting that Cotman's watercolor was the preliminary stage for a print (presently untraced). A Norwich artist, he went to London in 1782 and joined Thomas Girtin's sketching society. He was elected to an Associate Membership in the Watercolour Society, and in 1834, became the Drawing Master at the newly established King's College in London.

86. John Nash (1752-1835), attributed to
DESIGN FOR A COUNTRY HOUSE, ca. 1820-30

Watercolor, bodycolor, and pen and black ink over pencil, 9½ x 15 (23 x 37.8)
B1975.2.370

This edifice, erroneously called Longleat House, is an example of the Greek Revival at its most flamboyant. John Nash, often considered the most important architect of the period, designed Brighton Pavilion (1815) in the Indian style, Luscombe, Devonshire (1800) as a medieval castle and Cronkhill, Shropshire (1802) as an Italianate villa. This large, multi-columned structure is comparable in its lavish use of columns to Nash's Carlton House Terrace (begun 1827) and his Cumberland Terrace (1827), which also includes a central pedimented portico and several projecting columned bays.

87. George Shepherd (1770-1842)
VIEW OF A COUNTRY HOUSE AND CONSERVATORY, ca. 1820s

Watercolor over pencil, with surface scraping, 14¾ x 21¼ (37.2 x 53.8)
B1975.2.626

The Italianate villa style and stucco exterior of the house date in the early decades of the nineteenth century. As indicated here and in the plan for Middleton Park (Cat. 82), the influence of the landscape architects Humphrey Repton and John Loudon had instigated a return of the flower bed to the garden and stimulated interest in new and exotic strains of plants and trees. The large vaulted conservatory to the left of the house suggests that the owners were unusually devoted to horticulture, since few private residences had greenhouses of this size. Less elaborate conservatories were added to many houses, frequently serving as passageways between old and new parts of the house. Other innovations of the period are the trellis and large windows on the ground floor, which reflect attempts to bring together the house and garden. The flower bed, geometrically organized in the seventeenth century, reappears here with an irregular outline.

Shepherd, a native of Herefordshire, studied at the Royal Academy and occasionally exhibited there from 1811 to 1830. He was a landscapist who drew many views of houses and the scenery in Surrey, Sussex, Middlesex, and Kent.

88. William H. Bartlett (1809-1854)
CHATSWORTH HOUSE, DERBYSHIRE, ca. 1823-30

Pen and brush and brown ink over pencil, 6⅜ x 9¾ (16 x 24.3)
B1975.2.213

This drawing shows the north and west facades of Chatsworth house, constructed between 1696 and 1707. William Talman is known to have executed the south front (Cat. 62); the pedimented west front is of doubtful authorship but the curved north facade is considered to be the work of Thomas Archer.

The house was remodelled around 1818 by the 6th Duke of Devonshire. The north wing was added and the gardens were changed to a more formal appearance with parterres and fountains. The pedimented west front looked out over a walled area containing small, closely clipped beds of flowers and a central fountain included on the far right.

Bartlett was well known for his sketches and was employed in drawing views in England and abroad. He travelled to the continent and to Asia and America. About one thousand of his drawings have been published in such works as *Forty Days in the Desert* (1848), *The Nile Boat* (1849) and *The Pilgrim Fathers* (1853). This drawing probably dates to his early career from 1823 to 1830, when he was in England sketching important buildings and local scenery.

89. Anne Rushout (ca. 1768-1849)
VIEW OF SEZINCOTE, GLOUCESTERSHIRE, 1824

Inscribed, in brown ink, *Sezincot[sic] 1824,* lower right
Watercolor over pencil, 6⅞ x 10½ (17.4 x 26.7)
B1977.14.9506-9587

Rushout's watercolor spans two pages in her sketchbook, which includes seventy-seven drawings, a number of them on double pages. Her view shows the famous Indian-inspired house whose garden was painted by Thomas Daniell (Cat. 35). Samuel Pepys Cockerell built Sezincote for his brother Charles Cockerell about 1805. He based the exterior on Daniell's drawings of the Mausoleum of Hyder Ali Khan in Laulbaug (or Lollbaug) in northern India (Christopher Hussey, "Sezincote-I," *CL* 85 [May 13, 1939]: 505). Orientalizing elements on the exterior include multifoil arches, a deep bracket cornice, and onion domes. The house was set into an English landscape park scattered with caves, temples, and cascades to evoke an Indian locale.

Anne Rushout, the eldest daughter of the 1st Lord Northwick, is best known for her painted views of Northwick Park.

90. Cornelius Varley (1782-1873)
HARTWELL, BUCKINGHAMSHIRE, 1833

Inscribed in pencil, *July 18, 1833 C. Varley,* lower left; *South,* lower left; *east,* lower right
Pencil and grey wash, 14⅜ x 21 (36.1 x 53.4)
B1975.2.162

This house is located near Aylesbury about forty miles northwest of London. Originally built during the Tudor period by Sir Thomas Lee and his son, the house was enlarged in the mideighteenth century. The south and east fronts, shown here with their columned porticos, were built by Sir William Lee, Bart. between 1759 and 1763. The east front, designed by Henry Keene (1726-1776), combines a rectangular Tuscan porch with coupled columns and upper windows with pediments and Dutch style simple volutes at the sides.

Cornelius Varley, known chiefly as a watercolorist, was also a scientist and inventor. One of the founders of the Watercolour Society, he also made improvements on the *camera obscura* and the microscope.

91. Edward Jones (active 1819-35)
DESIGN FOR AN ATHENIAN VILLA, 1834

Inscribed, in black ink and grey wash, *Athenian Villa,* upper center; in black
   ink, *Perspective View shewing the Principal and Garden Fronts,* lower
   center; in brown ink, *April 28th 1834.,* lower right; *Edwd. Jones/ 67
   Great Russell Street/ Bedford Squ/ London,* lower left
Pencil and watercolor, 11½ x 17½ (29.2 x 44.5)
B1975.2.679

Greek-inspired designs such as this one typify interest in the
archaeology of antiquity which began in the 1750s and reached a
peak in England in the early nineteenth century. The fascination
with Greece gave rise to new fashions in architecture, interior decoration, furniture design and dress. Characteristic examples of the
Greek style are William Wilkins's Downing College, Cambridge
(begun 1806), and Robert Smirke's Covent Garden Theatre (1818-
19, burned 1856).

Although Jones visited Greece in the 1820s, when he made
sketches, this version of the temple form is not closely based on
ancient designs; rather it is a free and picturesque adaptation of the
Greek style. In the early nineteenth century, the "villa" came to have
a suburban connotation, and small houses in Greek, Gothic and
Italianate styles were built outside London for the professional classes.

92. British School XIX century
ROUNDWAY HOUSE, DEVIZES, WILTSHIRE, ca. 1840-45

Watercolor over pencil, 18 x 28 (45.5 x 71.5)
B1975.2.391

Roundway was a park area near the village of Devizes. The
land and the three houses associated with it were owned by the
Nicholas family from the thirteenth century to sometime after 1770,
when it was sold to the Willey family. In 1780, James Sutton began
to rebuild one of the Nicholas houses from designs by James Wyatt
(1747-1813) (see Cat. 76 and *Lee Priory,* Cat. 32). The old brick house
of the early eighteenth century was covered with stucco and enlarged
to form a hollow square around a courtyard. This view shows the
garden facade to the south, with awnings on the windows to block
the strong light. The wing to the left contained reception rooms.
The bow front projection is typical of Wyatt's style.

93. C.J. Richardson (1806–71)
DESIGN FOR AN ELIZABETHAN HOUSE, ca. 1840–60

Signed, in red ink, *C.J. Richardson—*, on mat, lower left
Pencil, watercolor, and body color with some gold paint, and pen and
    brown ink; revised insets by the artist on house, left, 11⅜ x 16⅞
    (28.9 x 42.8)
B1975.2.638

Among the many revivals of the early nineteenth century,
Tudor and Elizabethan styles were perhaps the latest to flower.
Interiors were redesigned in what was then thought to be the Tudor
taste, and furniture was made to simulate sixteenth and seventeenth-
century prototypes. A designer and architectural draftsman,
Richardson illustrated and published *Studies from Old English Mansions, their Furniture, Gold and Silver Plate* (1841) and *Picturesque
Designs for Mansions, Villas, and Lodges* (1870). The present drawing
may have been intended as the model for an illustration to one of his
books. It is a fanciful version of an Italianate stone house of about
1600 with a tower, ornamental strapwork, latticed windows and a
small formal garden in the rear. Figures in early seventeenth–century
costume stand at the left to complete the picturesque image.

94. Thomas Cubitt (1788–1855), ?Office of
OSBORNE HOUSE, ISLE OF WIGHT, ca. 1845

Watercolor, 29¾ x 51¾ (75.5 x 131.5)
No. 5131

Queen Victoria bought Osborne House in 1844 to use as a
summer retreat. It was decided to rebuild the existing structure,
creating a royal pavilion to house the private apartments and an
adjoining block to contain the larger state rooms. When completed
in 1848, the house was widely illustrated and frequently imitated in
England and America. Not only houses, but also town halls, railroad
stations and seaside hotels took their inspiration from Victoria's
"cottage" on the English Channel.

Osborne was remodelled as an Italianate villa by Prince
Albert, who dictated the design of the house and who was influenced
by the work of Sir Charles Barry at Trentham and Walton. The
belvedere tower, open loggia and seaside setting give the house a
Mediterranean flavor. Its builder, Thomas Cubitt, was known less
as an architect than as a real estate developer in London. He was

responsible for much of the development of Bloomsbury and Belgravia. This large and finely detailed perspective view of Osborne was probably intended as a presentation drawing.

95. Sir Charles Barry, R.A. (1795-1860)
DESIGN FOR TOWLEY MANOR, ca. 1845-50

Watercolor, bodycolor, pen with black and brown ink, and pencil, 11⅜ x 17⅛ (28.8 x 43.3)
B1975.2.361

Following the trend set by John Nash (see Cat. 86), Barry developed a rural Italian style for country houses which became popular in the mid-nineteenth century. Queen Victoria's Osborne also reflected this phase in English domestic architecture (Cat. 94). The landscape design for Towley (location and owner unknown) includes elaborate waterworks, cascades and terracing reminiscent of Italian sixteenth- and seventeenth-century gardens.

96. *William Lawson, fl. 1618*
A NEW ORCHARD, AND GARDEN: OR THE BEST WAY
FOR PLANTING, GRAFTING . . .

London: Printed by W. Wilson for John Harrison, 1648
Issued as part VI of Gervase Markham's *A way to get wealth*, London:
B.A. [i.e., Bernard Alsop] for John Harrison, 1648
Shown: Page 13: [Plan of an ideal garden]
Woodcut
Loaned by Beinecke Rare Book and Manuscript Library

This book is one of the earliest garden manuals devoted to
both the practical and decorative aspects of gardens and gardening. It
was first published in 1618 and appeared in several subsequent
editions prior to this one. Methods of fruit picking and planting of
trees, the destruction of caterpillars, and the raising of beds not
simply for aesthetic reasons but for proper drainage as well, are
carefully explained.

Lawson, a practicing gardener for over forty-eight years,
believed that the functional and formal aspects of the garden could be
integrated to appeal to all the senses. His book records early artistic
ideals of the terraced garden space. The plate shown is a three-tiered
or terraced garden similar to that of Llannerch (see Cat. 1).

97. Johannes Kip (1653-1722), after Leonard Knyff (1650-1722)
NOUVEAU THEATRE DE LA GRANDE BRETAGNE . . .

London: Joseph Smith, 1724
Shown: Plate 75: *"The Prospect of Notting-ham, From the East."*
Engraving by Kip after Knyff; *L. Knyff Deli*, lower left; *I. Kip. Sculp.*, lower
   right.

This is one of the French editions of *Britannia Illustrata, or
Views of several of the queens [sic] palaces, as also of the principle [sic] seats
of the nobility and gentry of Great Britain*, first published in 1707 as a folio
size book containing a series of engravings by Kip after drawings by
Knyff. These works, popular both in England and on the Continent,
were important picture books for country house owners who could
see the latest trends and innovations in architecture and garden
design. The book may have been used as a pattern book but more

likely it provided inspiration and ideas to those aspiring to own a country house.

In addition to Mr. Pierrepont's house shown here (see Cat. 11), Hampton Court, Herefordshire (Pl. 50; Cats. 4, 5, and 6) and Wollaton Hall (Pl. 68; Cat. 3) are also depicted in the edition.

98. Colen Campbell (d. 1729)
VITRUVIUS BRITANNICUS; OR, THE BRITISH ARCHITECT . . .

London: the Author [etc.], 1715 [-71] 5 vols.
Shown: Vol 3 (1725), Pl. 89
Elevation of Atherton in the County of Lancaster the seat of Richard Atherton Esqr. Design'd by Wm. Wakefield Esqr. 1723
Engraving *H: Hulbergh Sculp,* lower right; *Cai Campbell delin,* lower left

Vitruvius Britannicus is made up of five folio volumes with one hundred engravings in each, published in 1715, 1717, 1725, 1768, and 1771. An important source material of Palladian architecture for architects and patrons planning construction of country houses, the work contains plans, elevations and sections of both public and private buildings in England from the seventeenth and eighteenth centuries.

The book is open to a view of Atherton Hall as planned by William Wakefield, although Devis's painting of the house (Cat. 16) shows that the scheme was modified.

Artist and Country House Index

Numbers refer to catalogue entries

96

Plates

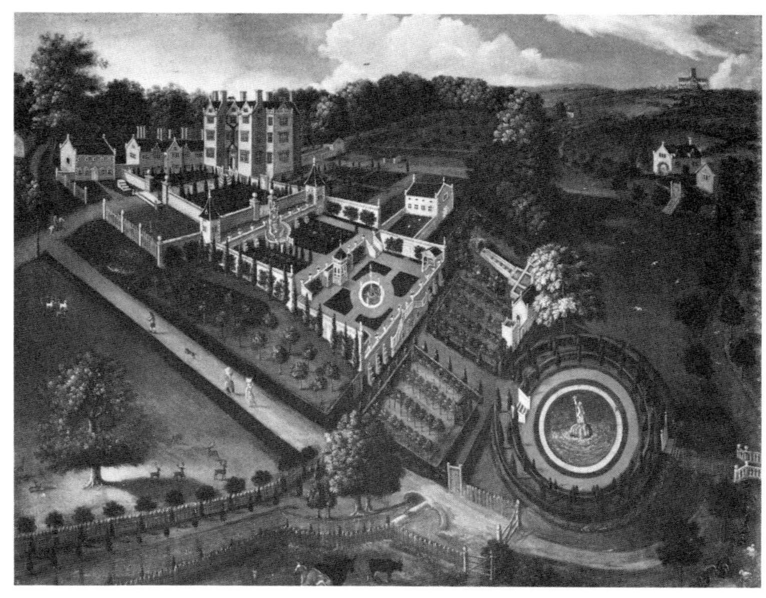

1. British School, XVII Century, A VIEW OF LLANNERCH, DENBIGHSIRE, ca. 1662-72

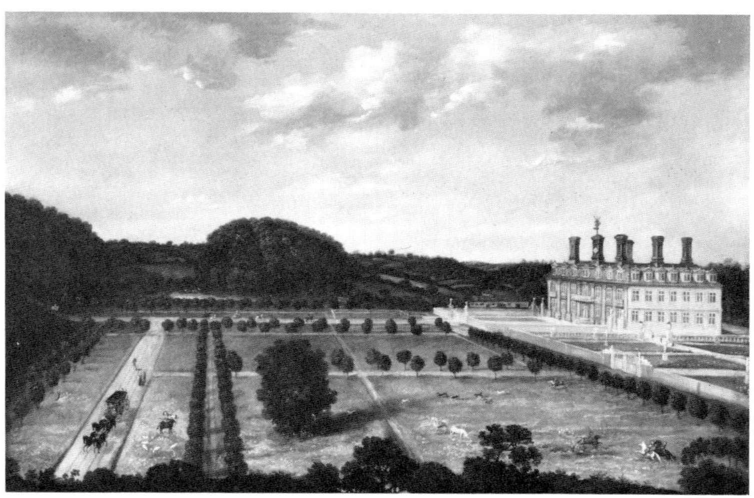

2. Jan Siberechts, A VIEW OF BAYHALL, PEMBURY, KENT, ca. 1675-85

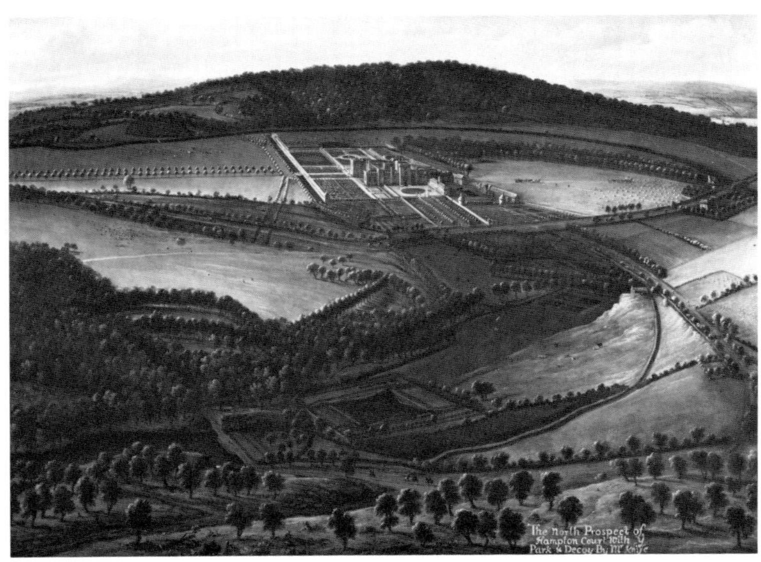

4. Leonard Knyff, THE NORTH PROSPECT OF HAMPTON COURT, HERE-FORDSHIRE, WITH PARK AND DECOY, 1699

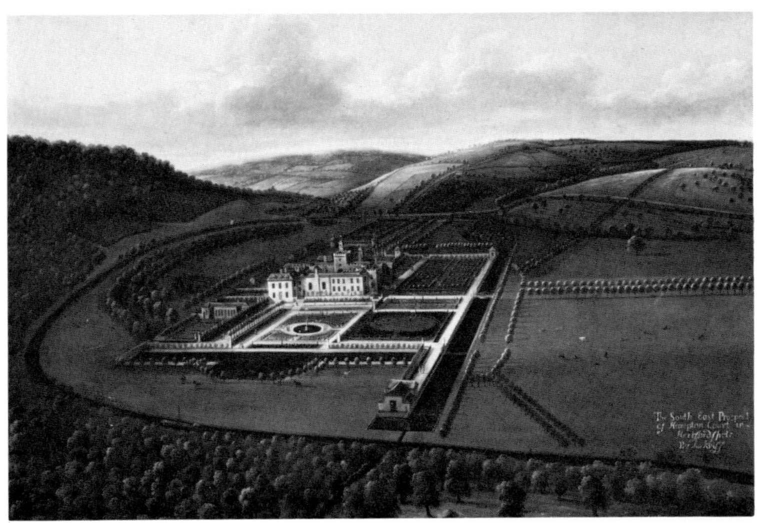

5. Leonard Knyff, THE SOUTHEAST PROSPECT OF HAMPTON COURT, HEREFORDSHIRE, ca. 1699

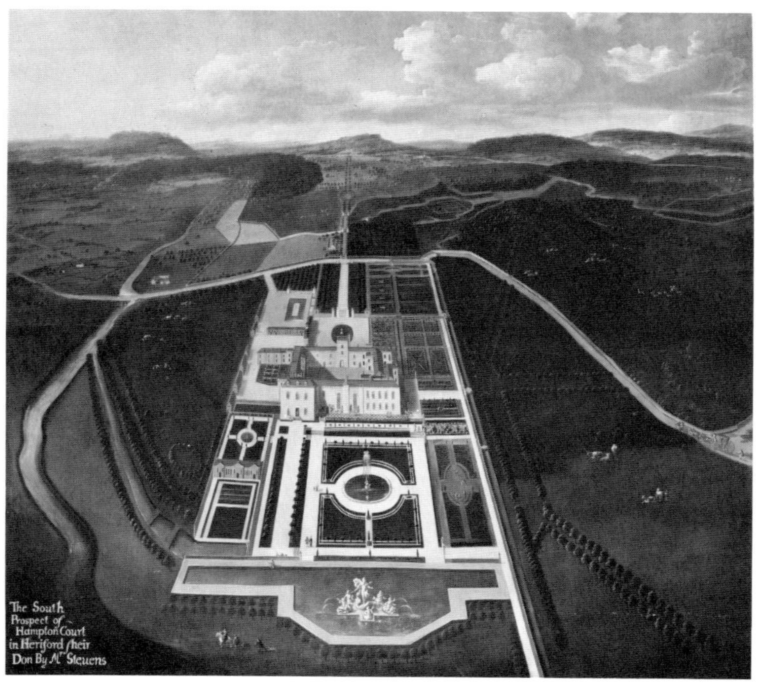

6. John Stevens, SOUTH PROSPECT OF HAMPTON COURT, HEREFORD-
SHIRE, ca. 1706–10

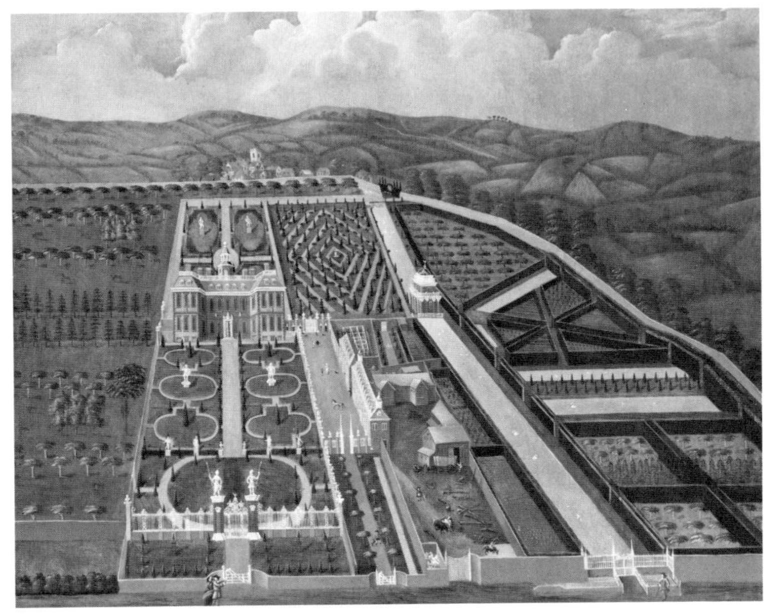

7. British School, XVII Century, A PERSPECTIVE VIEW OF DENHAM PLACE, BUCKINGHAMSHIRE, ca. 1695

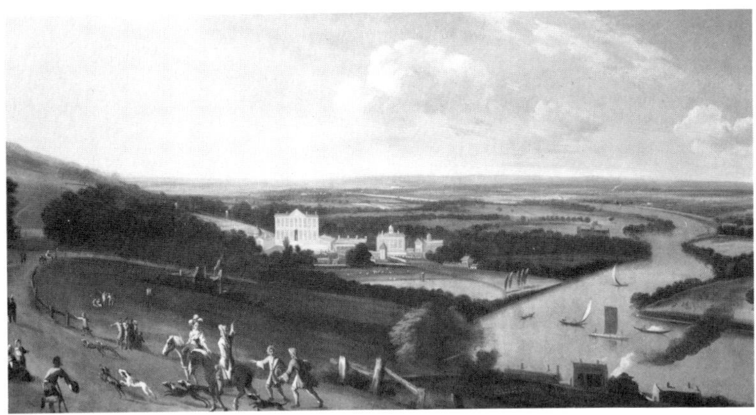

9. British School, XVIII Century, THE EARL OF ROCHESTER'S HOUSE, NEW PARK RICHMOND, SURREY, ca. 1700–1705

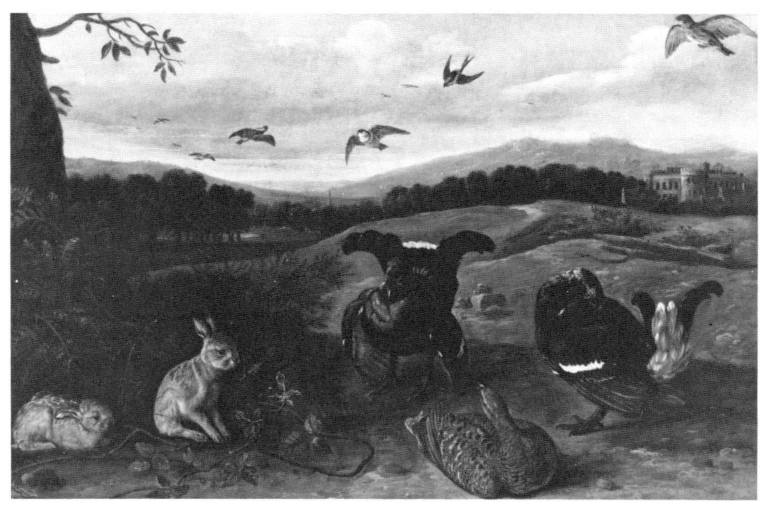

8. Leonard Knyff, BLACK GAME, RABBITS, AND SWALLOWS IN THE PARK
OF A COUNTRY HOUSE, ca. 1700

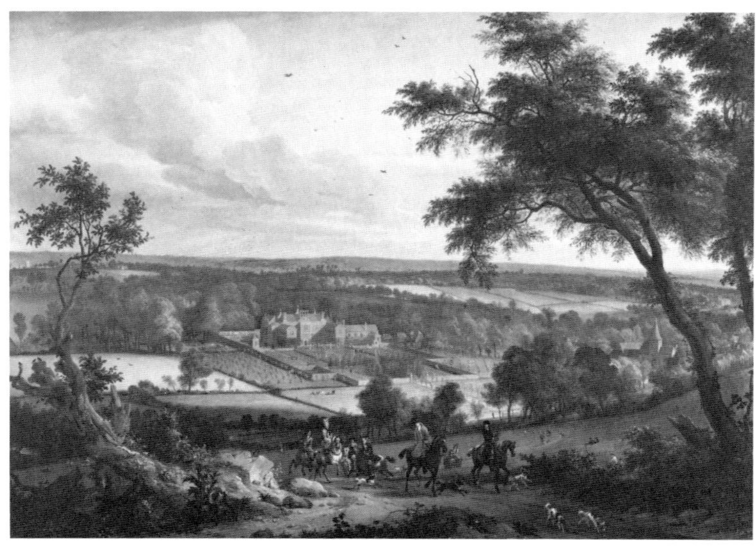

10. British School, XVIII Century, BIFRONS PARK, KENT, ca. 1705-10

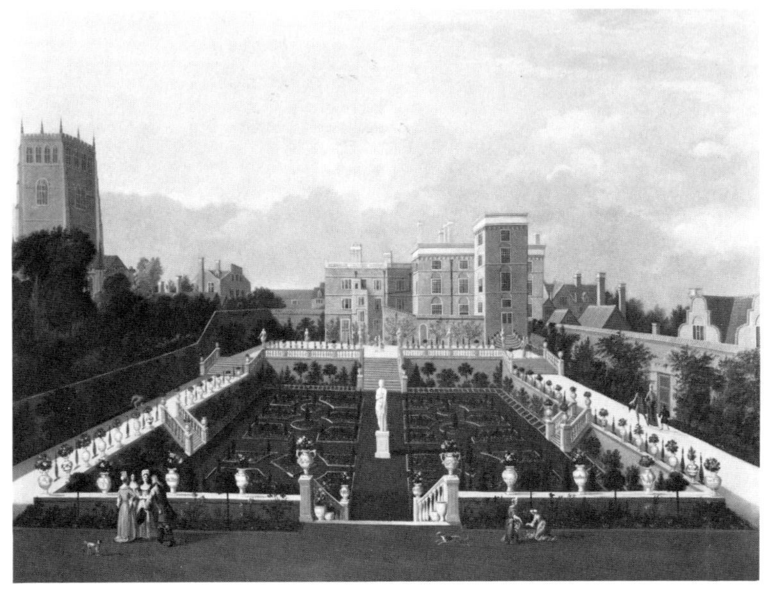

11. British School, XVIII Century, PROSPECT OF THE PIERREPONT HOUSE, NOTTINGHAM, ca. 1708–13

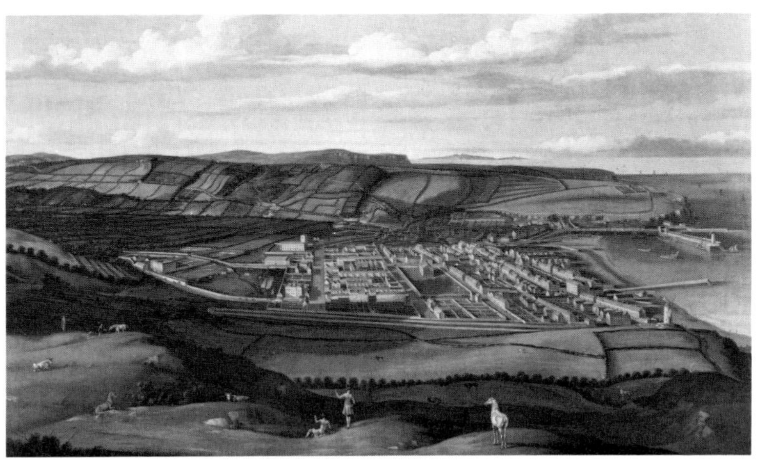

12. Matthias Read, PROSPECT VIEW OF WHITEHAVEN, CUMBRIA, SHOWING FLATT HALL, TO THE LEFT, ca. 1730–35

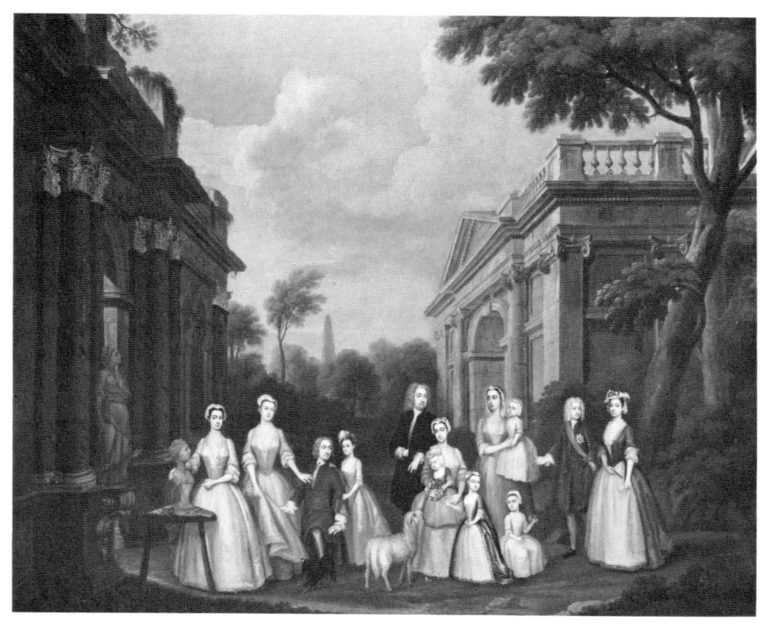

13. Charles Philips, THE FINCH FAMILY, ca. 1731-32

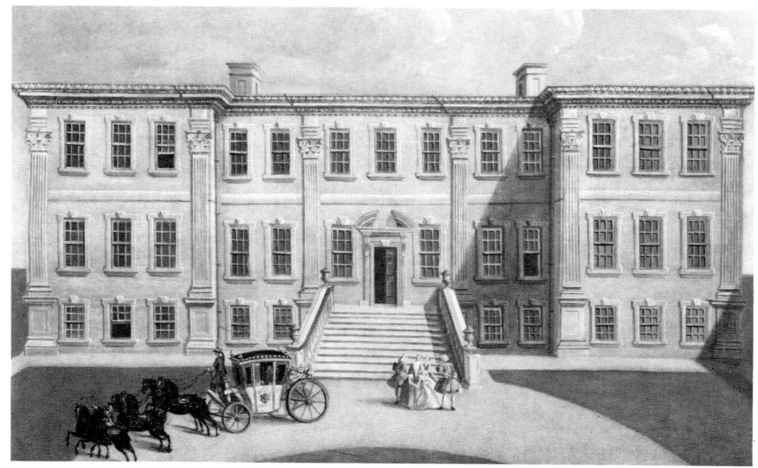

14. British School, XVIII Century, CALKE ABBEY, DERBYSHIRE, ca. 1734

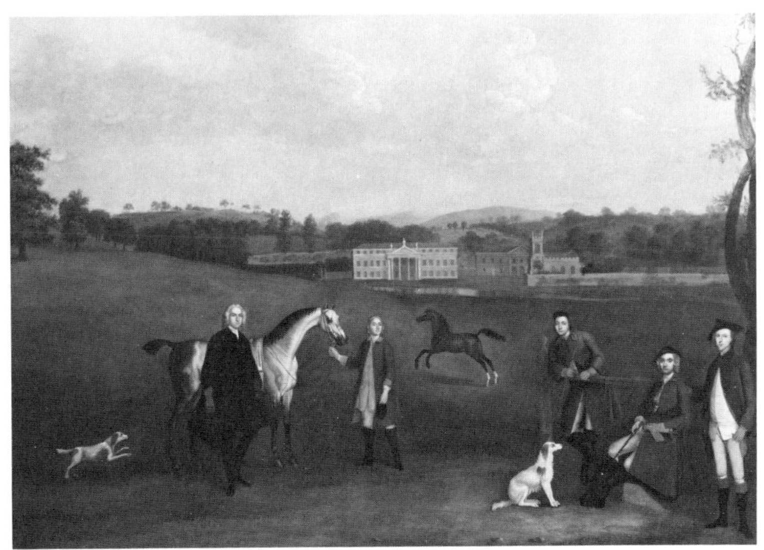

15. Arthur Devis, and an Unknown Artist, possibly James Seymour, LEAK OKEOVER, REV. JOHN ALLEN, AND CAPT. CHESTER IN THE GROUNDS OF OKEOVER HALL, STAFFORDSHIRE, ca. 1745-47

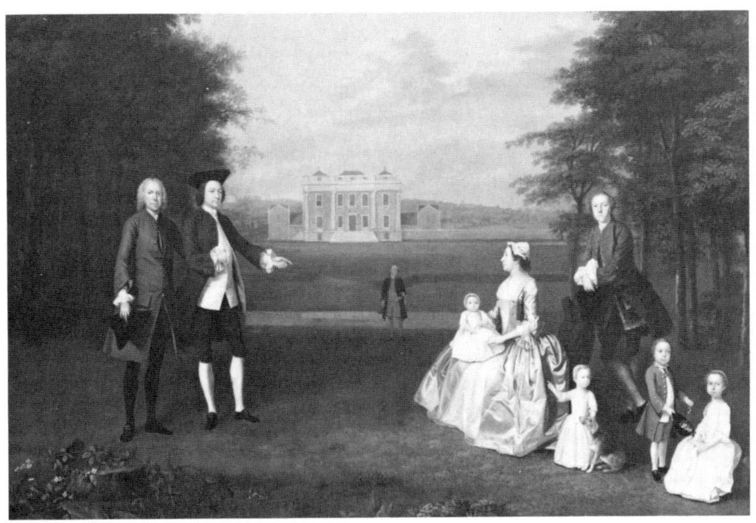

16. Arthur Devis, ROBERT GWILLYM AND HIS FAMILY AT ATHERTON HALL, LANCASHIRE, ca. 1745-47

108

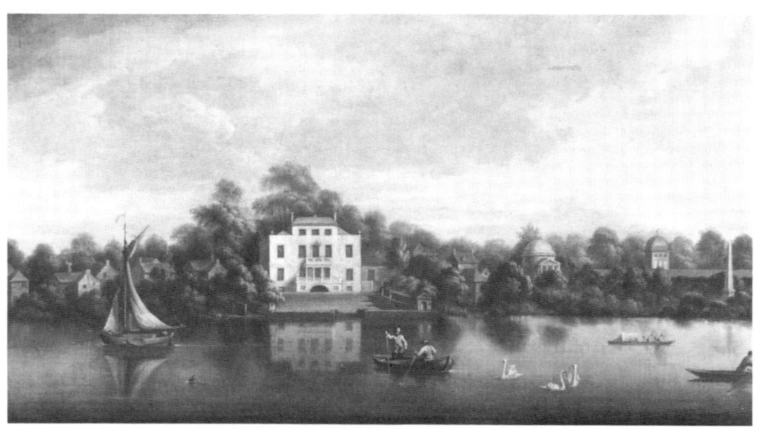

17. John Nickolls, ascribed to, POPE'S VILLA, TWICKENHAM, ca. 1755

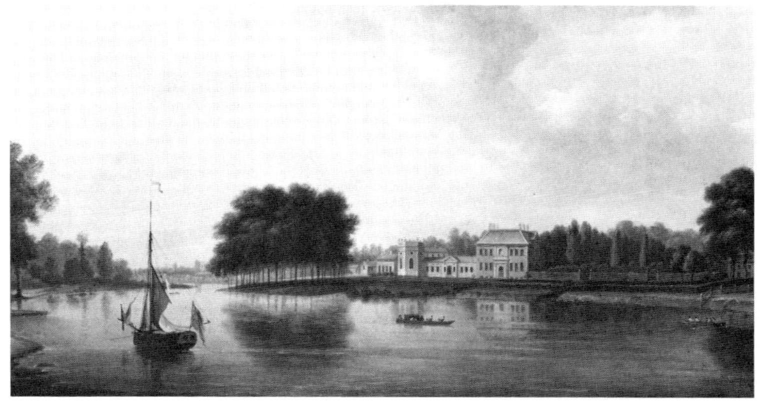

18. John Nickolls, ascribed to, ORLEANS HOUSE, TWICKENHAM, ca. 1755

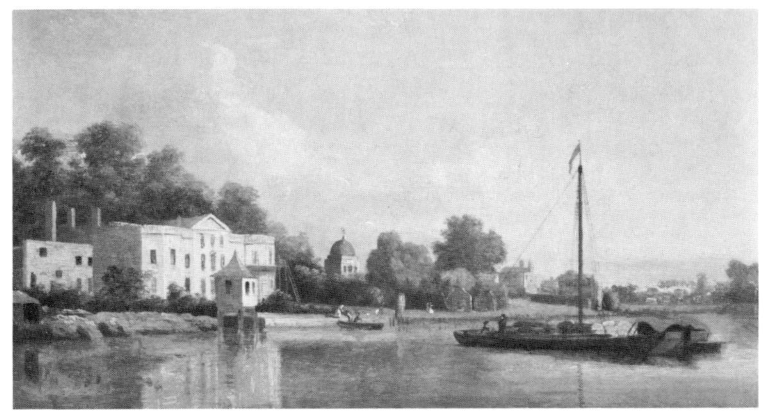

19. Samuel Scott, POPE'S VILLA, TWICKENHAM, ca. 1759

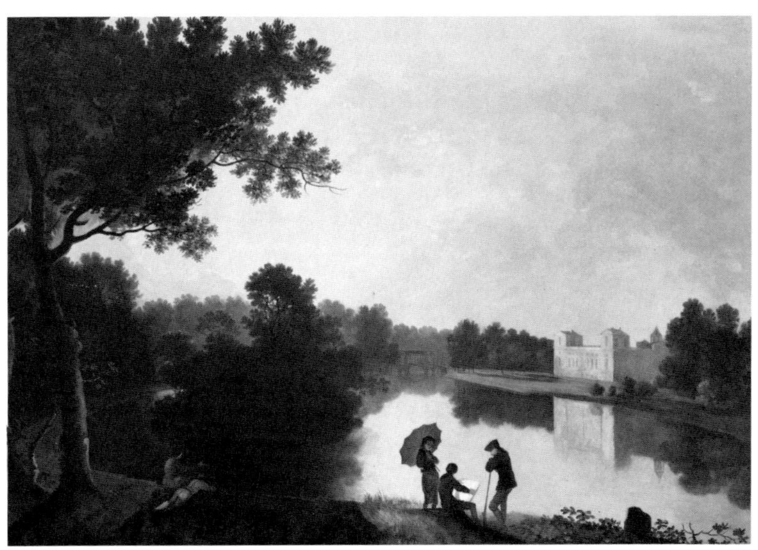

20. Richard Wilson, WILTON HOUSE, WILTSHIRE, FROM THE SOUTHEAST,
ca. 1760.

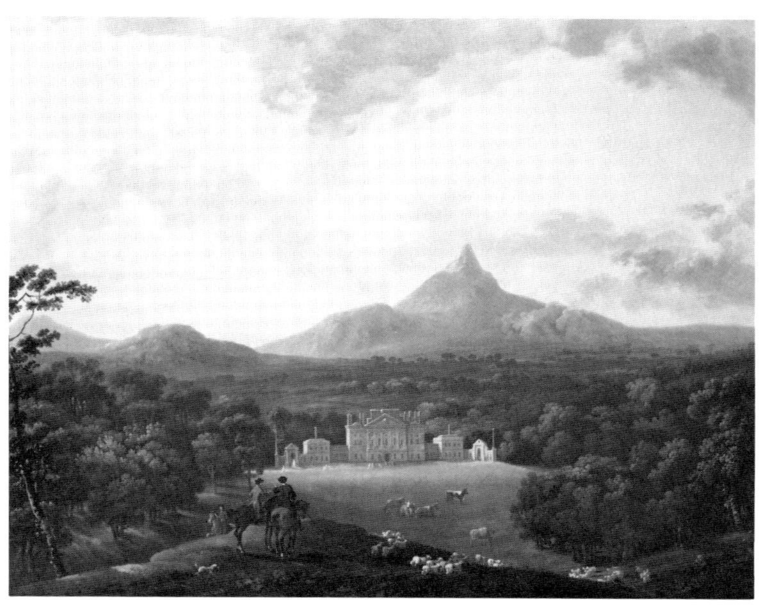

21. George Barret, Snr., A VIEW OF POWERSCOURT, COUNTY WICKLOW, IRELAND, ca. 1760-62

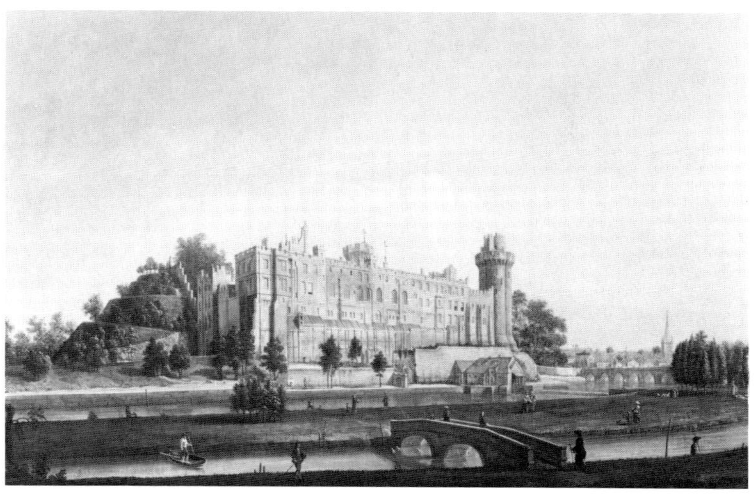

22. Francis Harding, attributed to, A VIEW OF WARWICK CASTLE, ca. 1764

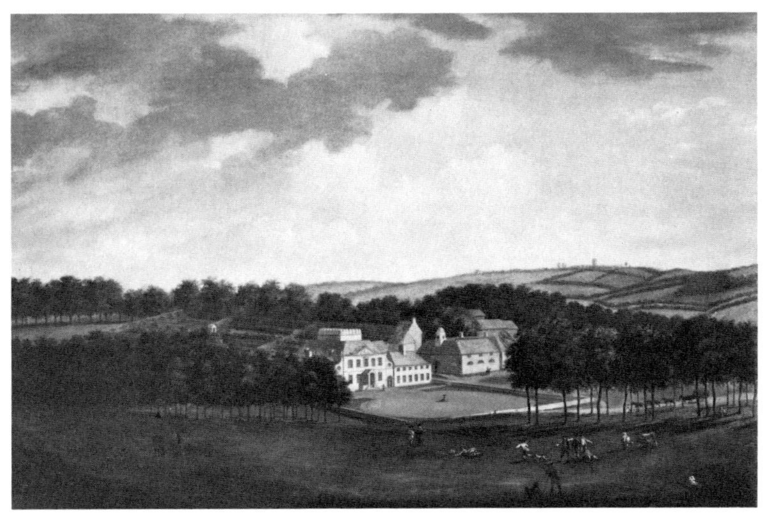

23. British School, XVIII Century, KIDBROOKE PARK, KENT, ca. 1770

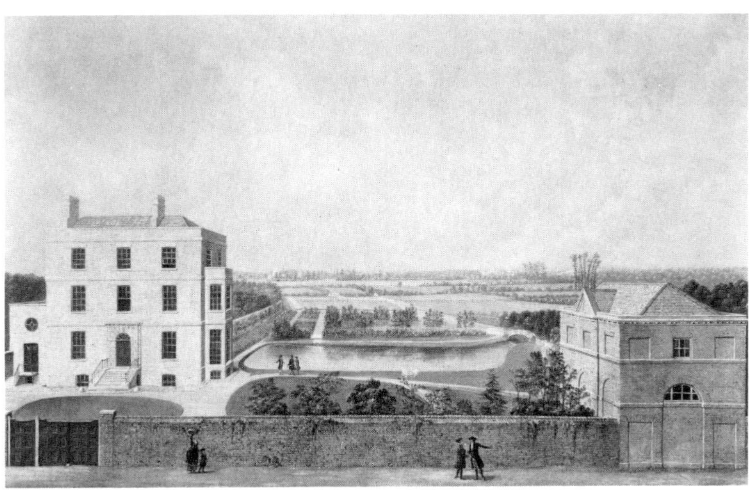

24. British School, XVIII Century, possibly Theodore De Bruyn, THE HERMITAGE, ca. 1770-76

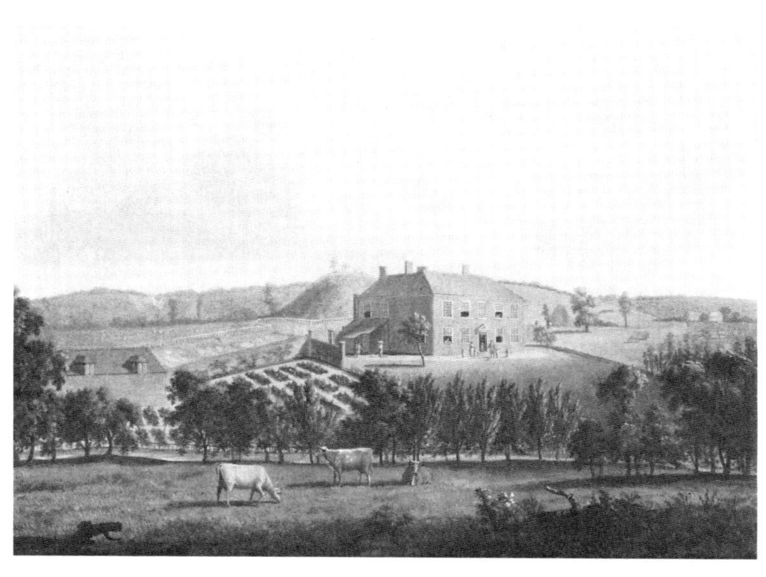

25. Dominic Serres, SAINT VINCENT, KENT, THE SEAT OF CAPT. WILLIAM LOCKER, ca. 1779-80

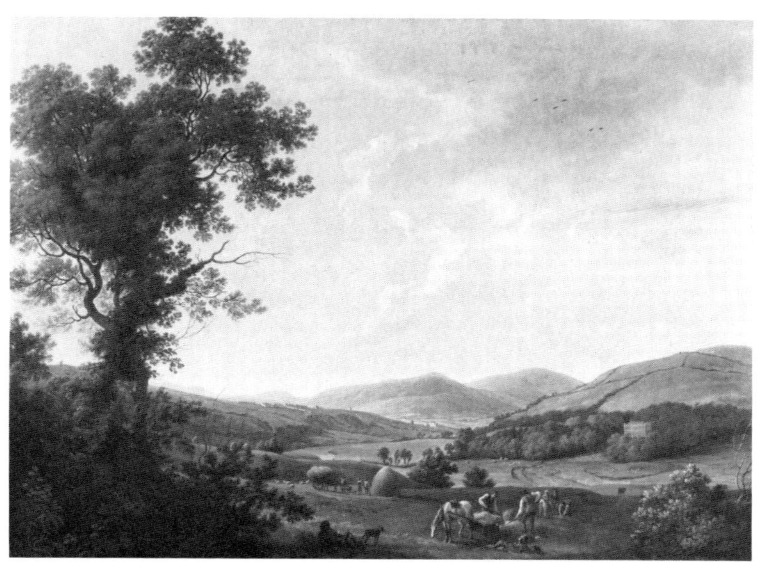

26. William Ashford, GEORGIAN HOUSE IN A LANDSCAPE, ca. 1775-80

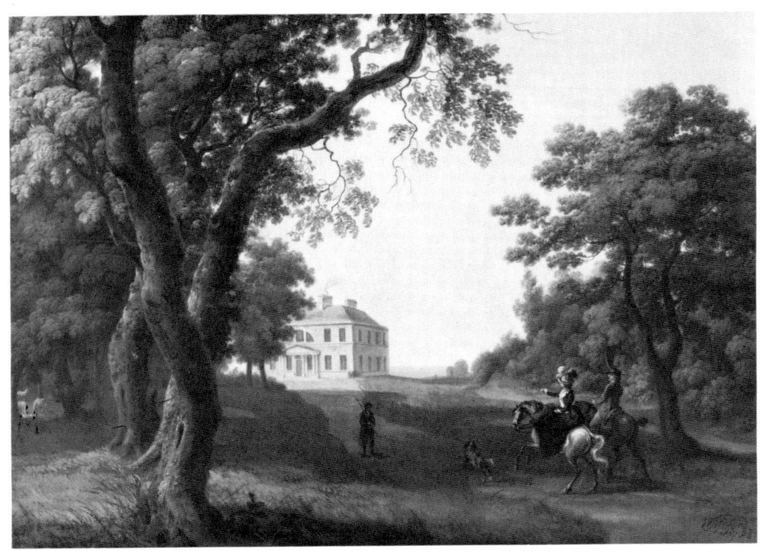

27. William Ashford, MOUNT KENNEDY, COUNTY WICKLOW, IRELAND, 1785

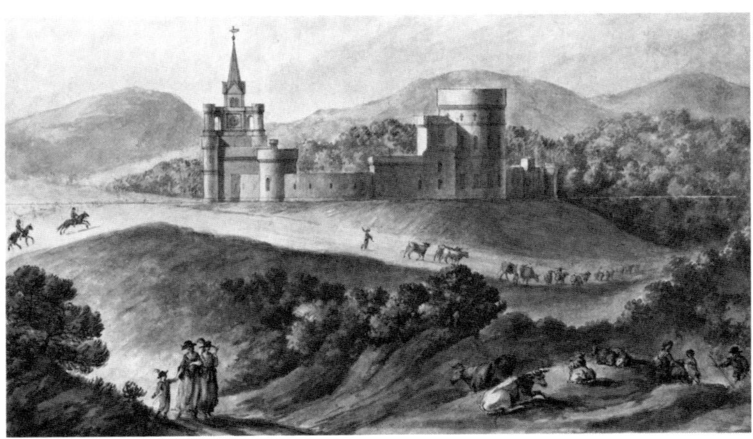

63. Robert Adam, A CASTELLATED COUNTRY HOUSE IN A LANDSCAPE, ca. 1775-85

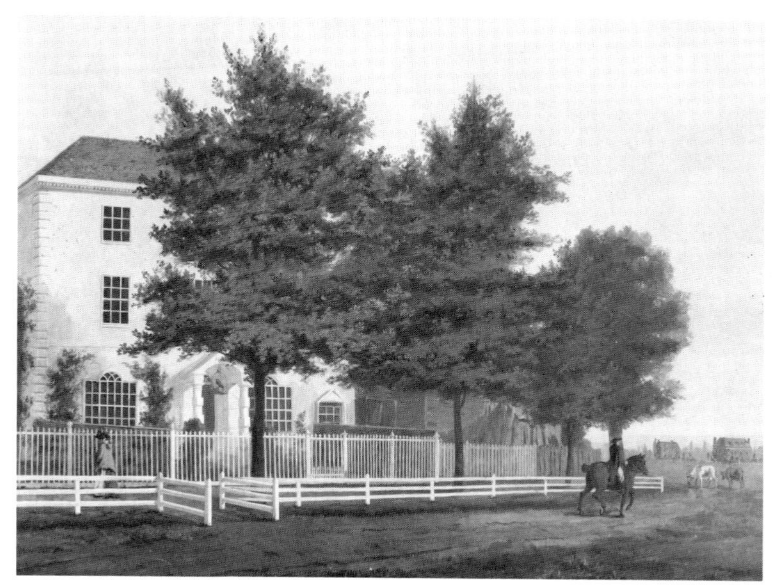

29. William Marlow, attributed to, GEORGIAN HOUSE ON A COMMON, ca. 1785-94

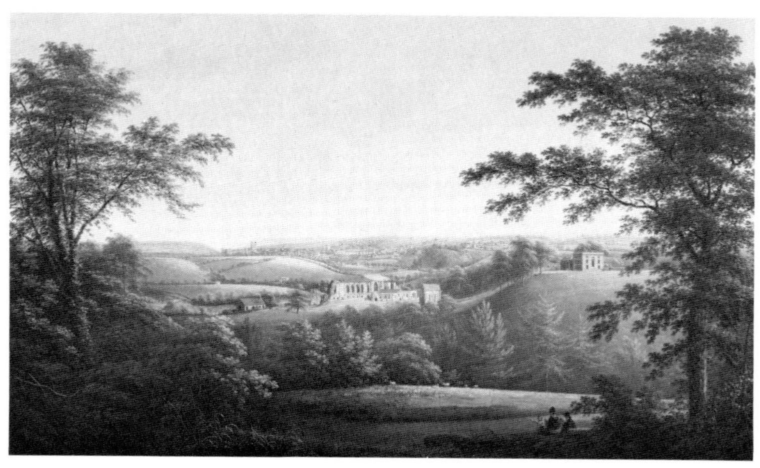

30. George Cuitt, Snr., VIEW OF EASBY HALL, EASBY ABBEY, AND THE PARISH CHURCH WITH RICHMOND, YORKSHIRE, IN THE BACK-GROUND, ca. 1790-1810

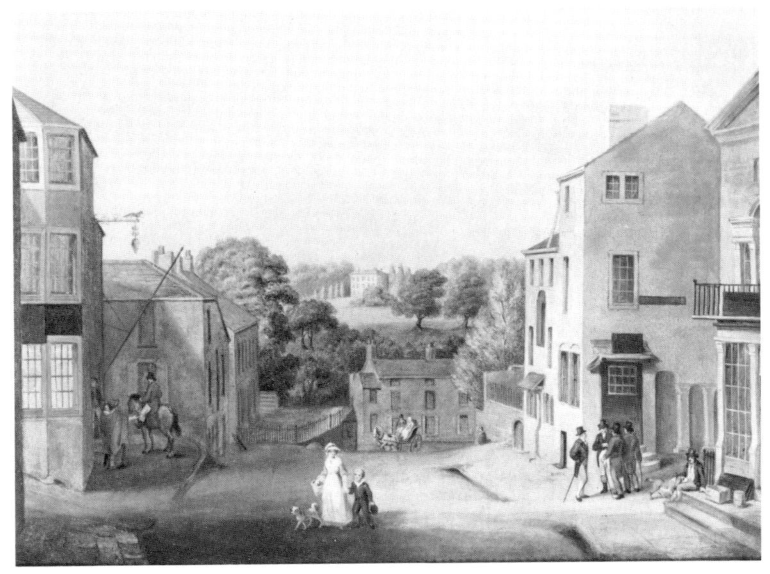

31. John Bird of Liverpool, STREET SCENE IN CHORLEY, LANCASHIRE, WITH A VIEW OF CHORLEY HALL, ca. 1790-1817

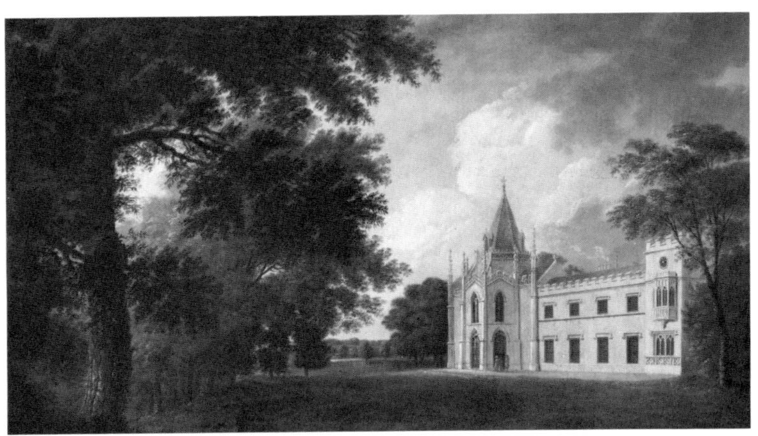

32. British School, XVIII or XIX Century, LEE PRIORY, KENT, ca. 1800

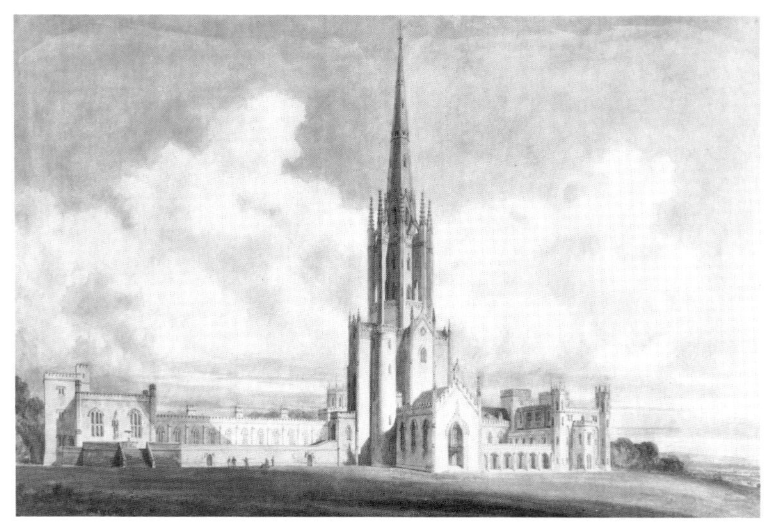

73. James Wyatt and J.M.W. Turner, A PROJECTED DESIGN FOR FONTHILL ABBEY, WILTSHIRE, 1798

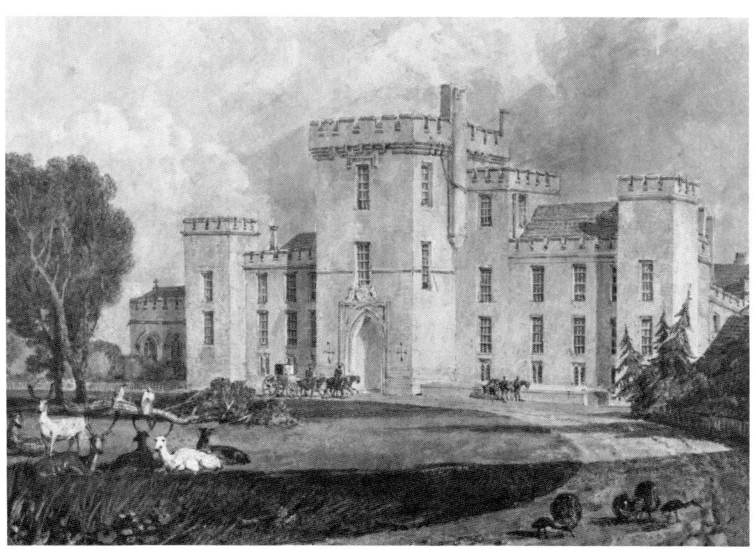

78. Joseph Mallord William Turner, A VIEW OF HAMPTON COURT, HEREFORD-SHIRE, FROM THE NORTHWEST, 1806

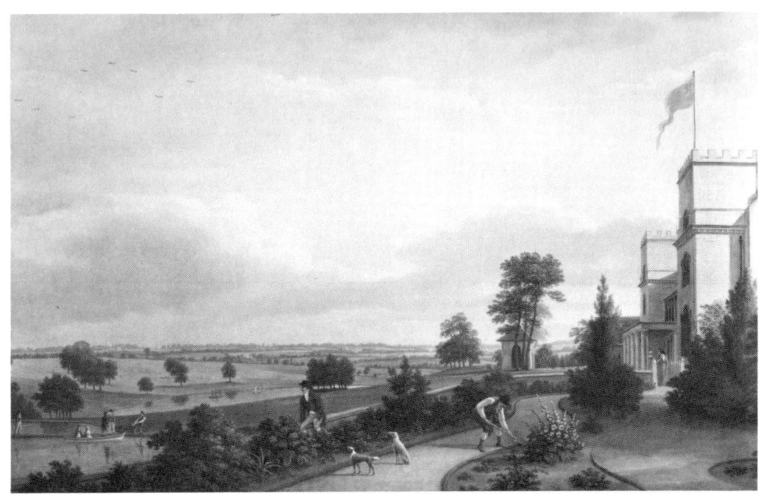

34. British School, XIX Century, COUNTRY HOUSE IN A RIVER LANDSCAPE, ca. 1800–12

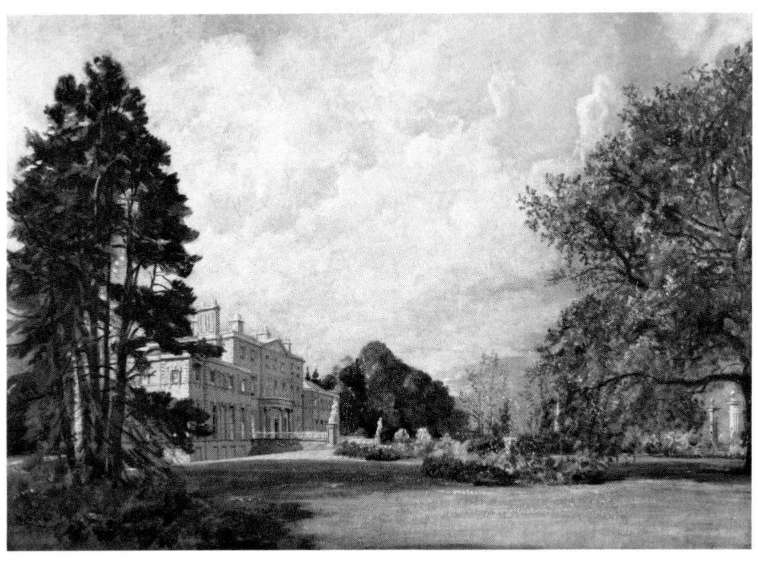

36. John Constable, MALVERN HALL, WARWICKSHIRE, ca. 1821

118

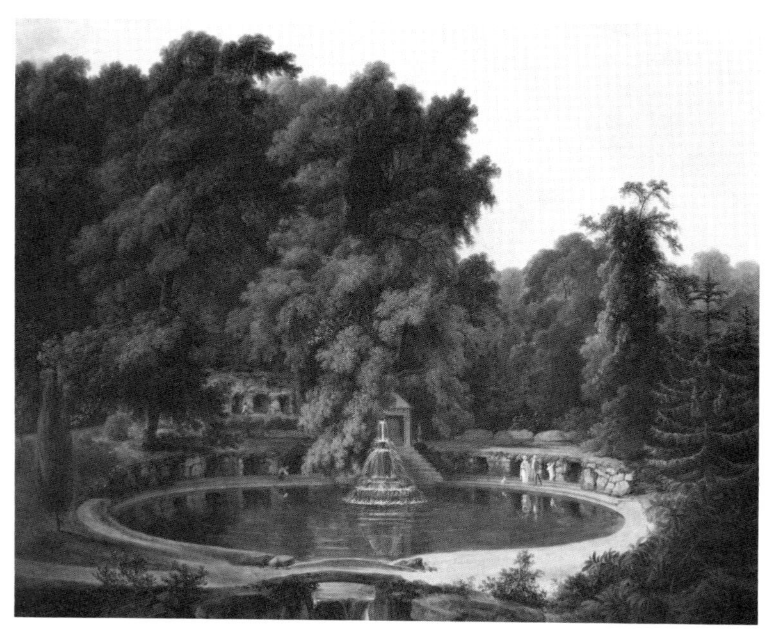

35. Thomas Daniell, A VIEW OF THE TEMPLE, FOUNTAIN AND CAVE AT SEZINCOTE PARK, GLOUCESTERSHIRE, 1819

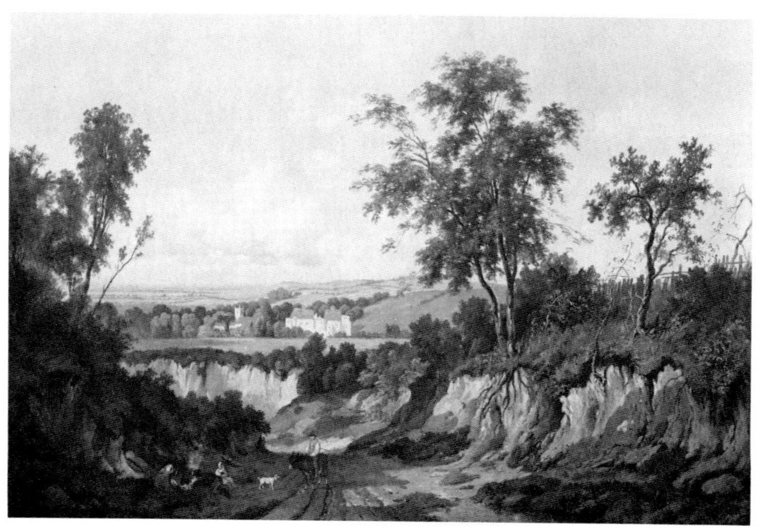

37. Patrick Nasmyth, PENSHURST PLACE, KENT, ca. 1824-30

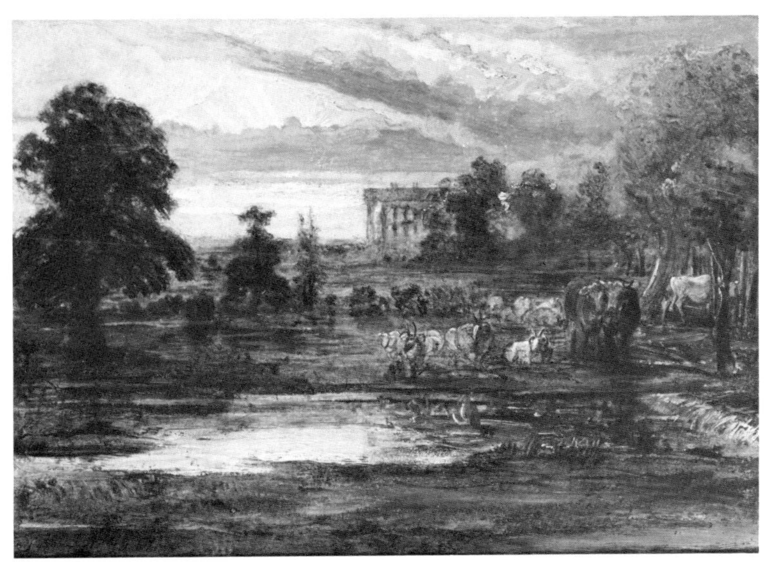

38. James Ward, CATTLE AT A POOL AT SUNRISE, 1827

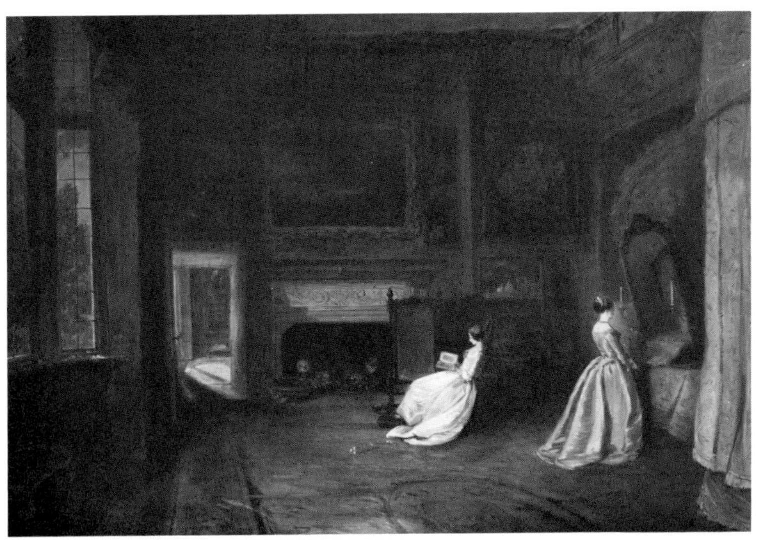

40. James Holland, THE LADY BETTY GERMAIN BEDROOM AT KNOLE, KENT, 184[?5]

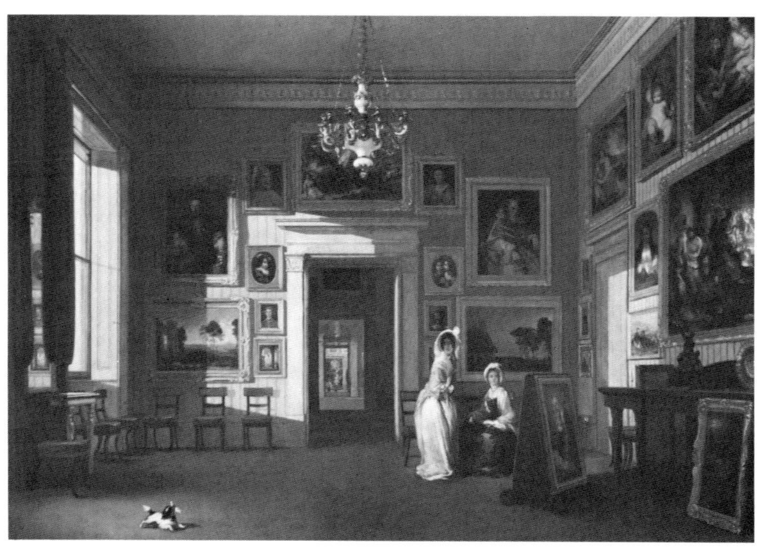

41. R. Huskisson, LORD NORTHWICK'S PICTURE GALLERY AT THIRLE-STAINE HOUSE, GLOUCESTERSHIRE, ca. 1845-47

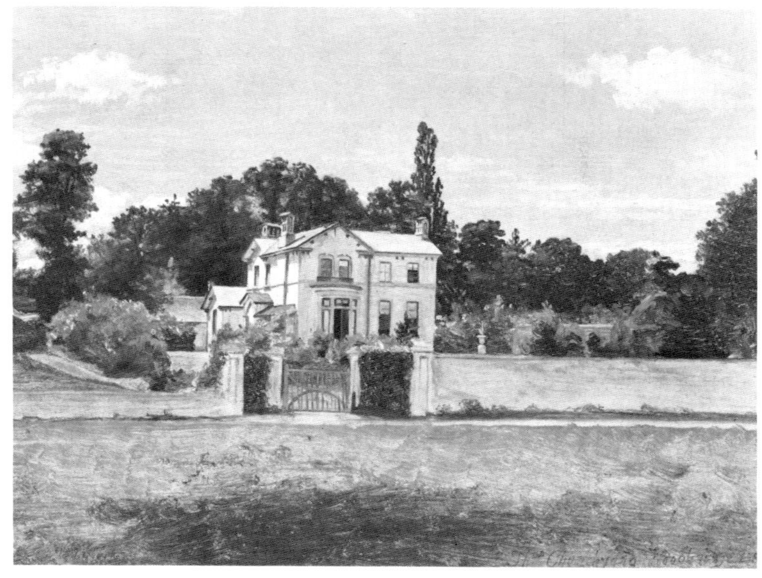

42. Thomas Churchyard, A HOUSE IN WOODBRIDGE, SUFFOLK, 1859

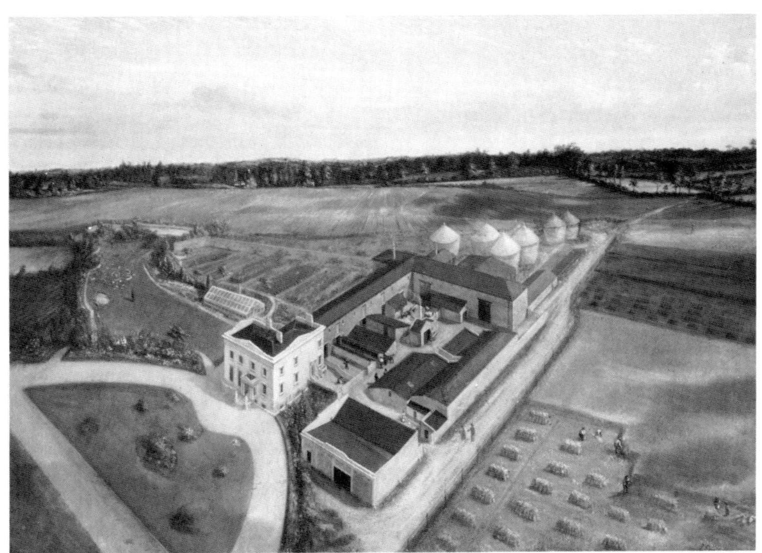

43. William Brown, attributed to, TIPTREE HALL AND FARM, ESSEX, ca. 1850-60